TESTIMONIALS FROM COUPLES WHO HAVE EXPERIENCED BREAKTHROUGH BY APPLYING THE PROCESS IN THIS BOOK

"We can't stress enough what the Sams have done for us. We were in a bad place before we met them, looking into divorce attorneys. But the Sams showed us a new perspective, God's view of us and what our marriage could be with effort and work. We were BOTH willing to put this work in, and it has paid off 10-fold. Today we are very happily married. We are grateful for each other and having the other in our lives. So grateful to the Sams for helping us reach the 'happy ever after' we both wanted."

—Jeff & Alissa Paulson (professionals)

"We were living together in body only. There was no relationship at all. We struggled desperately with how to communicate about everything. We would just get angry with one another and shove everything under the rug. Nothing was ever dealt with. We were like 2 porcupines living together…we were at beyond trying to make the marriage work. We are now communicating with each other. We are spending more quality time with each other. We are not going to bed angry. We are closer to each other intimately as well…before we came we were not intimate at all, not even holding hands. We now do bible study and prayer together which is the first time we have ever done that in 28 years of marriage. You have given us tools to deal with the present situations that we face now. Thank you so much."

—**Gino & Jan Paonessa (business owners)**

"We both wanted to avoid divorce and God in His mercy directed us to call Pastor Jeeva and Sulojana. Frankly, we didn't think they could turn our marriage around. We had seen so many ministry couples just fall apart and we dreaded the fact that were headed there too. We praise God that we were wrong!! Today, we are closer as a couple than we have ever been! Our relationship and intimacy has gone to a way deeper level. We are forever grateful for a new lease on life for our marriage!"

—**A couple in pastoral ministry**

"Our marriage was at the point of breakdown, and we were considering divorce. We couldn't seem to find the way out and had talked to counsellors, gone for individual therapy, and couples therapy, but nothing seemed to work. We are together today because of Jeeva and Sulojana and their teachings! They tackled our problems in marriage on a spiritual, emotional and physical level and taught us that healing has to occur at each level. We went back to the basics and began to rebuild our marriage. Our lives have been transformed though their marriage mentorship process. We've learned how to listen to each another, attack the issues, not the person, and live like Christ in our marriage. Jeeva and Sulojana have taught us that there is a solution to every problem, nothing is impossible, and nothing is beyond repair."

—**A couple in itinerant ministry**

"Before mentorship, there was a lack of communication, criticizing, discontent, defensiveness and stonewalling in our marriage. We had love for each other but would find ourselves in one of these categories on the daily. Christ wasn't in the centre, even though this was a goal of ours. Now we are more Christ-centered. There's open communication; we don't feel criticized or become defensive. We now also have communication and reconciliation tools, if needed, to overcome any problems that we may have."

—**A newly married couple**

"We were dealing with issues that we could not resolve on our own: broken communication, past hurts, unforgiveness and trust issues. We are grateful for Pastor Jeeva's and Sulojana's godly wisdom and prayers that sustained us throughout the program. We are working to communicate better because of the inner healing we received and the reconciliation tools that we were taught. Our relationship was like a rocking boat about to sink and we didn't expect a turnaround in our marriage."

—Dayanand & Irene Jacob (arranged marriage)

"We were like two ships passing in the night. There was little emotional connection. We were more like roommates than lovers. The coldness in our marriage brought great sorrow and fear that we would not make it in the long run. We both were conflict avoiders because of our past. There were areas where we had built walls and kept each other out. Our priorities were not in the right order. We also needed to have better prioritization of our time so that Jesus could truly be at the center of our marriage. Now we are more in-love than ever! We are truly happy! We protect each other's hearts, we prioritize and honour each other! We are stronger than ever! Jesus is truly now at the center. We are healed, healthy and whole!"

—K.S. & G.S. (second marriage for both)

"There was a wall between us and it was growing bigger every day. We were really struggling with communication issues and conflict resolution. Both of us had levels of hurt that we carried into our marriage. We wore protective armour around our hearts that didn't allow the other person to get through on an emotional level, which then affected the physical side of our relationship as well. We were approaching a point of no return, where if we didn't get help immediately, the marriage likely would not have survived. Our lines of communication are open and we are free to truly communicate with each other—choosing to hear first, before being heard. Both of us have experienced so much healing in our hearts that we view each totally differently. We turn to prayer first in moments of difficulty or crises and have active strategies to deal with conflict in a healthy way. There is a fresh joy and peace in our home that we haven't quite experienced before."

—T.K & K.K. (ministry leaders)

...AND COUPLES WHO RECEIVED PREMARITAL MENTORSHIP

"We both grew up in different cultures with different upbringings and coming together as one would be a challenging task, at least at the start. We wanted to explore premarital counseling to help us prepare to build a marriage on solid ground. We entered the marriage mentorship program with the Sams, and it was life changing. Not only did this program prepare us for the life we were about to enter into, but also taught us things that we did not know about ourselves that we needed to deal with before coming into communion with one another. It helped build a core foundation for our marriage and gave us tools to fall back on when we run into conflict. We are very thankful for the Sams and all that they have done for us."

—Manly and Sttefani Danh

"We had been living together for a number of years. Our main issues all involved lack of communication and the inability to resolve conflict in a healthy way. We had also grown apart in many ways and found narrowing the gap between us grew harder each day. We had run out of ideas on how best to handle the situation on any given day. Our new life in general is very different. We still have our moments as most couples do, but we now have a number of healthy ways to handle those situations. We have some great foundational work that we can now fall back on. Any couple who really sticks to the lessons and daily habits would find it difficult to come out the other side unchanged."

—Gary Holgate & Madelyn Suiciak

"When we came to Sulojana and Jeeva, we were concerned if we would be ready for the trials of marriage ahead. We were wrestling with asking the right questions and attempting to understand or accept each other's past relationships and life experiences. As a result of their mentorship, Sulojana and Jeeva created a safe place for us to have those conversations and find healing where needed. We participated in 10 weeks of mentorship before our wedding day. We've been married for 3 years now, still grateful for the processes we learned."

—Dan & Jessica Meier

ENDORSEMENTS

Here is what leaders in the Body of Christ have to say about *The Unbreakable Marriage*

"Wow, wow, wow! If ever there was a practical book to take a couple step by step through the various issues of marriage, this is it! We have had the joy of knowing Jeeva and Sulojana for 15+ years. We've been a part of their spiritual journey. We know their amazing children. We have seen the development of their skills as marriage coaches. We too have benefited from their marriage mentorship as we had them personally help our marriage using the various skills that are laid out in this wonderful book. They have a guarantee that couples who go through the steps in this book will have a restored marriage. We affirm that guarantee!"

—**Steve & Sandra Long**
Senior Leaders, Catch the Fire Toronto

"*The Unbreakable Marriage* is PERFECT! What we mean, having done marriage counseling for other couples—is that this book seems to have it all! Simple enough that couples in their 20's could easily grasp each concept; comprehensive enough that those married for only one year or for 40 years could each glean new and marriage-healing information from, and advanced enough that those at a university could use this same book while receiving college credits. This book is for pastors, parishioners, home groups, marriage-healing groups, or just the curious couple about to be married who truly seek a roadmap for marital happiness and even married bliss! Get this book and while you're at it, buy one for a friend too!"

—Steve and Derene Shultz
Founders: THE ELIJAH LIST & ELIJAH STREAMS!

"*The Unbreakable Marriage* is chocked full of time-honored practices for ways to build and protect strong marital connections! The Sams are ready to take you on a journey of healing and freedom in these pages. As someone who has walked with thousands of couples through difficult times, serious disconnects and even the stress of normal life, I will highly recommend that you allow the Lord to supply you with the hope and nourishment contained in this book. I love the promise these two set out there, *"We guarantee breakthrough for married couples on the brink of breakdown in as little as 10 weeks"* because they know they can deliver with content like this! If you are serious about transforming the future of your relationship, then this is definitely the path for you!"

—Danny Silk
President of Loving On Purpose, Author of Keep Your Love On,
Unpunishable and Loving Your Kids On Purpose

"*The Unbreakable Marriage* by Jeeva & Sulojana Sam is a thoughtful and thorough look at what is required to have a successful marriage. They have covered every aspect of marriage—from communication to spiritual oneness to intimacy and managing conflict. You will find this book a great encouragement, whether you are struggling in your marriage or simply need to grow in your life-long relationship. Every couple should read *The Unbreakable Marriage*."

—**Os Hillman**
Author, TGIF Today God Is First

"Having been married for over 40 years, we understand the importance of working through issues so that the blessings of long-term covenant can be experienced and enjoyed. In *The Unbreakable Marriage*, Jeeva & Sulojana Sam detail a unique process that is solidly Scriptural and totally Spirit-led which has been producing breakthrough for the couples they have been mentoring for the past 5 years. They challenge couples to get to the internal roots of their problems first before applying external solutions. The real-life examples they share, combined with the action steps for every segment make this book a practical guide for couples to see results right away. You will be blessed by their wisdom, humour, honesty and vulnerability. We are pleased to commend The Sams and *The Unbreakable Marriage* as valuable resources to the Body of Christ."

—**Wesley & Stacey Campbell**
wesleystaceycampbell.com

"The breakdown of marriages and families has led to monumental devastation in society. Yet, the Lord's heart is to not only heal but cause the arising of anointed marriages that accurately reflect the dynamic of how Christ loves His bride. Jeeva and Sulojana Sam have been effectively ministering healing to marriages for many years. Drawing from their experience, spiritual knowledge, and God-given gifting, they have written an excellent work in *The Unbreakable Marriage*. In unpacking Biblical truths, highlighting engaging stories and bringing practical advice, this book is sure to help broken marriages heal and bring mediocre ones into vibrancy."

—**John and Patricia Bootsma**
Catch the Fire USA National Outreach Directors

THE UNBREAKABLE MARRIAGE

HOW TO STAND IN UNITY AND WITHSTAND ADVERSITY

JEEVA AND SULOJANA SAM

THE UNBREAKABLE MARRIAGE:
How to Stand in Unity and Withstand Adversity

Copyright © 2022 Jeeva and Sulojana Sam

ISBN: 978-1-7780861-0-6

All rights reserved. Except for brief excerpts for review purposes, no part of this book may be reproduced or used in any form or media without permission from the publisher.

Any website addresses recommended throughout this book are offered as a resource to you. These websites are not intended in any way to imply an endorsement from the authors, nor do they vouch for their content. The information in this book was correct at the time it was published.

Names have been changed to protect privacy, except in testimonials, with permission.

All Scripture quotations, unless otherwise indicated, are taken from the Holy Bible, New International Version®, NIV®. Copyright ©1973, 1978, 1984, 2011 by Biblica, Inc.™ Used by permission of Zondervan. All rights reserved worldwide. www.zondervan.com. The "NIV" and "New International Version" are trademarks registered in the United States Patent and Trademark Office by Biblica, Inc.™

Scripture quotations marked NLT are taken from the Holy Bible, New Living Translation, copyright ©1996, 2004, 2015 by Tyndale House Foundation. Used by permission of Tyndale House Publishers, a Division of Tyndale House Ministries, Carol Stream, Illinois 60188. All rights reserved.

Scripture quotations marked TPT are from The Passion Translation®. Copyright © 2017, 2018 by Passion & Fire Ministries, Inc. Used by permission. All rights reserved. ThePassionTranslation.com.

Scriptures quotations marked GNT are taken from the Good News Translation – Second Edition © 1992 by American Bible Society. Used by permission.

Cover design by Hester Barnard. Graphic inspired by a vision God gave Steven Kasyanenko.
All other graphics designed by Krysta Koppel.
Typeset by Medlar Publishing Solutions Pvt Ltd., & Amit Dey, India.

DEDICATED TO

Our models of Unbreakable Marriage:

Jeeva's father, Rev. Dr. Edward Sam and mother, the late Mrs. Suganthy Sam who were blessed with 60+ years of marriage

&

Sulojana's father, the late Mr. Manuel Gnanamony, mother, the late Mrs. Ponnesam Manuel and stepmother, the late Mrs. Kanakam Manuel

and those for whom we are privileged to model an Unbreakable Marriage:

Our children:
Priya and her husband Duncan,
Sathiya and his wife Shaloma, and
Jaya and his wife Rachel

CONTENTS

Preface: Who Is This Book For? xvii

Introduction xix

Chapter 1: Fundamental Principles 1

Chapter 2: Assessing Your Marriage 15

Chapter 3: Shifting The Spiritual Atmosphere 21

Chapter 4: Removing Spiritual Blockages. 57

Chapter 5: Growing In Communication. 101

Chapter 6: Restoring Peace Following Conflict. 115

Chapter 7: Going Undercovers 133

Chapter 8: Making Time 161

Chapter 9: Marital Finances 169

Chapter 10: Boundaries. 185

Celebrate Your Unbreakable Marriage 199

A Blessing For Your Marriage. 201

Afterword: Where Do You Go From Here?. 203

Additional Reading & Resources. 205

Acknowledgments. 209

About The Authors 213

PREFACE: WHO IS THIS BOOK FOR?

This book came out of our experience of mentoring married couples on the brink of breakdown to breakthrough in as little as 10 weeks with a results-guaranteed or money-back offer.

If you are facing a marriage breakdown or if you are separated and considering divorce, the process we share in this book will provide you with hope, help and healing, if both of you are desperate for a breakthrough.

Our process is designed for BOTH husband and wife to work through together. Order a copy of the companion workbook from www.thesams.ca/resources (or scan the QR code below), find yourself a mentoring couple who will keep you accountable, and you will be well on your way to breakthrough.

Maybe you are not at the breaking point now, but you know that your marriage is in trouble and you realize that unless you do something right now, you are headed for a breakdown; or if you are newly married or engaged and admit that you need a strong foundation and framework to build a marriage that lasts "till death do us part", you too will benefit from what we share in this book.

For some of you, using this book and the corresponding workbook may be a good start, but not enough. You will need expert help to take you from breakdown to breakthrough. You can benefit from the personalized, customized mentoring options we offer. Please visit www.thesams.ca.

INTRODUCTION

Never in our wildest dreams did we imagine that God would use us to help restore people's marriages when we got married in 1983 in the town of Martandam, about 45 km from the southern tip of India.

We had only met each other 10 days earlier. Ours was an arranged marriage in the Indian tradition where matches are made by parents, often with the help of a marriage broker. Parents entrust this go-between with a "shopping list" of their preferences, such as age range, education, profession, income level, faith, socio-economic background, physical appearance, personality, and character. The broker connects the parents of individuals in their inventory who appear to be suitable matches for each other, and the parents begin negotiations.

The ability of the bride's parents to offer a dowry is a significant determining factor for many of these matches. A dowry could be in the form of money, jewellery, household goods, property, or all of the above. In our case, the dowry was not a high priority; what mattered most were faith, character and education, in that order. Okay, to be fair, good looks and a pleasant personality were on the list as well.

A 15 Minute Courtship

Thanks to a hard bargain driven by our broker, our elders begrudgingly allowed us to meet for 15 minutes, alone, to talk about the things that mattered to us. Since many in India get married without ever having met their future spouse ahead of time, ours was viewed as an unconventionally *lengthy* courtship! After those 15 minutes, it was up to us to make our decision.

You are probably wondering how we could make such a life-changing decision in such a short time! Our courtship—as do most in India—stands in stark contrast to Western culture where much emphasis is placed on ensuring that you've found the right person before making the commitment of marriage. Co-habiting is often seen as a "trial marriage" to ensure that you can manage life together effectively.

In contrast, as children steeped in the Indian culture, we believed that since our parents knew us better than anyone else, they were more equipped than we were to find our spouse for us. They did the "background checks" on our behalf through family and friendship networks. We trusted, respected, and valued their judgment. An arranged marriage let us avoid all the hassle of chasing and catching a "perfect match" along with the broken hearts and bad dates that most people in the West experience as normal. This was our journey

INTRODUCTION

and we're not putting down the typical Western process of dating or courting. In fact, all three of our children found their spouses without an assist from us. Not that we didn't offer, of course.

Whether you found one another yourselves, or your parents set things up, the success of your marriage is entirely up to the two of you. It is not just about finding the right person to marry; it is also about becoming the right person for the one you married.

As odd as this may sound, we have also found that the feeling of being in love is not essential to having a loving marriage either. In his book, *The Chemistry of Love*[1], psychiatrist Mike Leibowitz explains that feelings of falling in love arise from a person's brain being flooded with a "love cocktail" consisting of numerous neurological chemicals. The euphoric high of love cannot be sustained long-term and is not necessarily even a requirement in the first place. There was no romance in the beginning for us. How could there be if we were strangers? We *chose* to love each other first and romance followed. For us, romance was

> **It is not just about finding the right person to marry; it is also about becoming the right person for the one you married.**

---

[1] *The Chemistry of Love.* Michael R. Liebowitz. Berkley Books.

not a pre-requisite for marriage. Love was a decision. Period. (*End of sermon!*)

What weighty matters do you think we discussed during our 15-minute courtship?

I (Jeeva) wanted to make sure that Sulojana knew what life was going to be like in Canada. We would have no help from anyone, no "maid service" as was common for middle-class families in India. I also asked her if she knew how to cook. She lied and said, "Yes."

In my (Sulojana's) defence, it wasn't exactly a lie. I knew how to boil an egg and I was confident I could learn how to cook other dishes while waiting the three months it would take for my Canadian visa to be approved.

We got married and went on a short honeymoon. A few days later, I (Jeeva) returned to Canada and began the immigration process for Sulojana. The hoped-for three months turned into

INTRODUCTION

nearly six before her visa was approved and she was able to come and join me.

This meant that I (Sulojana) had a longer grace period in which to learn how to cook. This worked in Jeeva's favour, although he did not see this delay as a godsend in any way. We wrote letters back and forth, as there was no telephone in our house. Periodically, Jeeva would call a local business at a pre-arranged time, I would go there, and we could only talk for a few minutes, as international long-distance phone calls were extremely expensive in the early 80's.

Married Life Begins In Canada

Our waiting finally ended on a cold wintry day in February 1984, when I (Sulojana) arrived at Regina Airport in Saskatchewan, Canada. It was quite a shock to my system, as it was about 90 degrees Fahrenheit colder than when I had boarded a plane in India. After spending the night at the home of our friends, Brian and Judy Moore, we headed off to the sprawling metropolis of Kincaid (population: 300) to begin our married life together as a couple.

About half-way into the 2.5-hour drive, I started getting concerned about my decision to leave everything behind in India and migrate to Canada. The landscape looked bleak, with hardly any people, houses, or businesses in sight. I could bear it no longer, and I turned to Jeeva and said, "Can I ask you a question?"

"Sure," he said.

"Where are all the people?"

He simply laughed and explained that we were now in the countryside where people lived on farms which were usually miles apart from each other. Being winter, there was no need for them to be outdoors. I was silent for the rest of the drive, processing it all in my head.

Finally, we arrived at our little house on the prairie which would be our first marital home. Once Jeeva taught me how to use Canadian appliances, I was off to the races and started cooking delicious Indian meals out of the thick book of handwritten recipes I had compiled during my six months of grace! As a side benefit, my arrival also increased the population of Kincaid to 301.

Our Share Of Ups And Downs

Our first year of marriage was a bit rocky. We did not know each other at all, so we were doing our "courtship" while already being married! Jeeva had become "Canadianized" during the eight years before I (Sulojana) arrived and had rather unrealistic expectations of how fast I would adapt to life in Canada. I also had to get used to my new status as a pastor's wife. The people of the church gave me the room to grow into the role, but I had to come to terms with my own expectations.

To complicate matters, my father passed away suddenly in India of a stroke, just six weeks after my arrival. I could not go back for his funeral and had to grieve without my birth

INTRODUCTION

family around me. Good news would soon follow, however, when I found out I was pregnant with Priya (we wasted no time). I had to contend with morning sickness for most of the pregnancy, but it was a small price to pay for the joy that her arrival brought us!

In 1985, we moved to Regina where our family grew further with the birth of our sons, Sathiya and Jaya. In 2003, we moved to St. Catharines, Ontario, just 15 minutes from Niagara Falls and the U.S. border, where we live to this day. We have been married for 38 years, as of August 18, 2021. I (Jeeva) retired from active congregational ministry after more than 35 years of service in 2017. Sulojana works full-time for the Government of Canada. Priya and her husband Duncan live in Toronto, about 90 minutes away. Sathiya and his wife Shaloma live just a few minutes from us, as do Jaya and his wife Rachel. What a blessing it is to have your adult children living close to you!

Over these years, our marriage has seen its share of ups and downs. As you will discover later in the book, we faced major struggles in two key areas—finances and sex. We went through medical challenges as well: I (Sulojana) underwent two major surgeries, we almost lost Sathiya at childbirth, and Jeeva had to contend with a giant polyp in his colon. By the grace of God, we overcame these challenges and even experienced a miraculous removal of the polyp without the need for the scheduled surgery! By the grace of God, the finance and sex-related struggles turned into victories, but these were hard-won battles.

Preparation For Mentorship

In 2010, "100 Huntley Street", a Canadian Christian television network, invited us and two other couples to walk through all 40 days of *The Love Dare*[2] and produce a daily video blog of the experience. We were chosen partly because of our uniqueness as a couple in an arranged marriage.

It was a great experience for us. Although we had been happily married for 26 years at the time, we drew much closer to each other. During that 40-day process, we would occasionally receive requests for help from couples going through a rough patch in their marriage. We would respond with a brief note of encouragement, sometimes dispensing advice, and always providing prayer—but we didn't consider ourselves marriage coaches by any means.

I (Sulojana) sensed at that time that God was calling us to work more closely with married couples who were in distress, but Jeeva dismissed the idea. Having worked in pastoral ministry his whole career, he didn't want us getting involved in the "life-sucking" drama of other couples' marriage problems. Being the supportive wife that I am, I went along with his sentiment, but I couldn't shake the sense that we were called to work with married couples. I believed in my heart that God would make it happen if it was His plan. Then I waited. And waited. And waited some more. Six years flew by.

---

[2] *The Love Dare* is a 40-day plan with a "dare" for every day that challenges husbands and wives to understand and practice unconditional love. It was instrumental in saving a marriage in the movie *Fireproof*. For more see: www.fireproofmymarriage.com

INTRODUCTION

Marriage Mentorship Is Born

In early 2016, five different men in leadership positions in businesses or churches contacted me (Jeeva) asking for help with their marriages, all within a six-week period. I couldn't say "No" anymore. We had no idea how to go about it, but it seemed it was time for us to start working with couples whose marriages were in deep trouble and in need of help to get back on track.

One thing God made clear to us is that we needed to do something different from conventional Christian ministry models of restoring marriages. Since we are not trained counselors or therapists, we could not call it marriage counselling. But we were more than coaches offering encouragement and strategy, so we did not want to use that term either. We sensed that one way we could help couples experience breakthrough was by becoming part of their lives in an intensely personal way for a short stretch of time. Since we could not move in with them or have them move in with us, the next best option was to offer 24/7 access to us for a short period of time, 10–12 weeks. We would meet with them in person or online once a week and do a mid-week check-up between sessions. This is how our marriage mentorship would differ from counselling or coaching, but what would the content be?

In April 2016 we were flying to Los Angeles from Toronto, when we sensed God starting to release ideas of what we should cover in our marriage mentorship. We jotted them down as quickly as we received them and rearranged them into an outline, which would become the basis of our curriculum.

Upon returning to Canada a week later, we made a short video about how our mentorship might be able to help couples in distress, and posted it on Facebook. One young couple responded right away, and we began the process together. Here is part of the testimonial we received from them:

> "I don't know where we'd be without Jeeva and Sulojana's ministry. My husband and I had become like roommates in a marriage focused outside our home, on our careers. Loneliness, rejection and resentment had built up a solid wall between us, and our well-intentioned attempts to make it work seemed increasingly feeble and forced. Our hearts had grown hard. In that vulnerable state, I developed feelings for a co-worker. We felt hopeless and we both considered we had made a mistake in our choice of partner. What could we do?
>
> We turned to Jeeva and Sulojana for help and are so glad that we did. The Sams provided effective, non-judgmental support at a critical time in our marriage. Their methods are solid. After an initial assessment—which was spot-on—they focused on spiritual care and helped us truly soften our hearts toward one another. When we had come to a place of healing, they trained us in more practical ways to make our marriage work.
>
> They made themselves available to us when we needed it and were generous with prayer. They kept their promise to take us from 'breakdown to breakthrough', and we are so grateful."

INTRODUCTION

The joy of receiving testimonials such as this and those in the opening pages of this book is the motivation behind the labour of love that you are reading. Over the course of a few weeks, by the power of the Holy Spirit and the process we took them through, this couple's marriage was restored. Not only are they still together five years later, they also have two beautiful children. Seeing pictures of their happy family brings us tears of joy every time we see them. With this early success, we were on our way to becoming Marriage Mentors.

Over the years since then, we have met many couples who were at the breaking point, hanging on by a slender thread of hope. We have wondered, at times, if some of them would ever get their breakthrough, before joyfully seeing their marriage become a *"rope made of three cords"* that is *"hard to break"* (Ecclesiastes 4:13 GNT).

What we will share in the pages that follow are the same steps we have used to mentor countless couples, helping them move from the brink of breakdown to breakthrough in as little as 10 weeks. We fully believe that when you take this message seriously and apply what we teach diligently, you too will put yourself in a place where the Holy Spirit can produce a testimony such as the one above.

We will begin by outlining some of the fundamental principles upon which our Marriage Mentorship Process is based.

CHAPTER 1

FUNDAMENTAL PRINCIPLES

YOU HAVE NO "MARRIAGE PROBLEMS"

This might seem an odd claim to make for a process aimed at helping married couples work through their problems. We can imagine some of you might be thinking:

"But we are barely talking to each other."
"We are always fighting with each other."
"We hate being with one another."
"We are not sleeping together anymore."
"We don't even want to touch each other."
"What do you mean, 'We have no marriage problems?'"

Hear us out: yes, you are facing some serious problems in your marriage. Otherwise, you wouldn't be reading this. We understand that. On the surface it may seem to you that the problems you are experiencing were produced by the two of you during your married life, in other words, they are "marriage problems." However, the roots of these problems almost always

> You have no marriage problems. You are two individuals with your own problems coupled together in a marriage.

lie beneath the surface in the hidden parts of our individual lives. Sure, you might benefit from some surface-level communication coaching, but that's not the real problem here. The real problem is that you are two individuals with your own deep areas of hurt and unmet needs.

Each of you brought your own lives into your marriage, including any history of traumatic childhood experiences, of parental neglect, of being abused by others, of witnessing unsafe anger, of shame, of fears and phobias, of failed relationships, unforgiveness and so on.

When the two of you—with your own problems—are coupled together in a marriage, it's only a matter time of time until you "give birth" to so-called marriage problems. If you try to solve these problems without addressing the unresolved individual issues beneath the surface, any results you do see are not likely to last. It's like cutting down a tree without removing or killing the roots—it might look like the tree is gone, but just you wait till next Spring!

When you each make the time to identify—and find the courage to address—the personal roots of your deep-seated issues, you will find yourselves to be a resilient couple who can confidently face any issues that arise in their marriage, with hope. That is why we say, "You have no marriage problems. You are two individuals with your own problems coupled together in a marriage."

Jim & Jane's Story

Jim and Jane came to us with a marriage that was rocky and shaky right from the get-go. Throughout their journey they had experienced emotional adultery, mental cruelty and loss of physical intimacy. To their credit, they did not keep their problems to themselves. They had already sought and received professional help, but they were still at each other's throats. There was more war than peace in the home. In desperation they turned to us for help.

At first, all they could talk about was how their problems stemmed from the way they had treated each other. They were both masterful at playing the blame game. Understandably, they saw one other through hurt-tinted lenses, but they were open to the idea that their problems went deeper than their own relational history. They even admitted that that they had entered into marriage with problems that went all the way back to their childhood and teen years.

Vulnerable honesty revealed a history of experiencing abuse, abandonment, condemnation, trauma, rejection, and violation of personal boundaries. They realized that these unhealed hurts which they brought into their marriage had continued to rear their ugly heads all through their married life. In other words, they were two individuals with their own problems who were coupled together in a marriage.

Through an intensive and thorough process of Spirit-led mentorship, they began to receive the healing they needed. The roots of their problems were identified and addressed. As healing came, festering open wounds began to close. Past hurts didn't simply disappear, but they lost their power to control Jim and Jane's behaviour. Today they are eagerly looking forward to spending the rest of their lives together.

Can you relate to Jim and Jane? What unhealed hurts or unmet needs might you have brought with you when you got married? This is not always an easy question to answer. Even thinking about it might bring up painful memories or even a feeling of panic. You may not even fully understand what has happened to you; you might just have a sense that you were impacted by something that someone did that felt disturbing or "off." Please take your time and do your best to write down all that comes to you at this time. If you're not able to identify anything, that's OK too. The Holy Spirit will reveal to you gradually all the things you are ready to deal with, as you keep on moving forward in this process.

No matter what your story is, no matter how bad and horrible parts of it may seem, there is hope for you. You too can receive healing for your hurts and learn to relate to one other with healed hearts, not out of the pain you are carrying today. Keep on reading, and keep on applying what you read, diligently, consistently, persistently. In time, you will learn how your own individual issues and problems have contributed to your marriage ending up in the state it is now. You will also learn how to ensure that those issues from your past do not adversely impact your marriage again.

FUNDAMENTAL PRINCIPLES

THE SPIRIT-SOUL-BODY CONNECTION

Couples who come to us for mentorship often see long-lasting results much faster than some other approaches to marriage restoration. We believe the primary reason for this is the holistic Spirit-Soul-Body approach that is one of our fundamental principles.

> *"Now may the God of peace make you holy in every way, and may your whole **spirit** and **soul** and **body** be kept blameless until our Lord Jesus Christ comes again"* (1 Thessalonians 5:23 NLT, emphasis ours).

The body or the physical part of our being is, of course, obvious to identify. It refers to what happens on the outside of our being—our words and our actions, our unspoken responses and our visible reactions.

The soul is the collective name we use to describe the mind, will and emotions. In some Christian circles, you may have heard people speak in negative terms about the realm of the soul, diminishing the importance of emotions, feelings, and so on. It is true that there are times when what we do with our mind, will and emotions is in opposition to what the Spirit of God would direct us to do, but it is God who created us with a soul. He gave us a mind, will and emotions as integral, good parts of our humanity. He has also given us the ability to determine what we do with our soul, as David illustrates in these two verses:

> *"Bless the Lord, O my **soul**; and all that is within me, bless His holy name!"* (Psalm 103:1 NKJV)

> *"Why, my **soul**, are you downcast? Why so disturbed within me? Put your hope in God, for I will yet praise him, my Saviour and my God"* (Psalm 42:11).

Acknowledging the reality of the soul and our ability to control our thoughts, emotions and will is key to receiving holistic breakthrough in your marriage.

The spirit is, we believe, the deepest part of our being, our core. It is at the spirit level that we experience the deepest possible communion with God. This is where our identity is revealed and sealed. *"The Spirit himself testifies with our spirit that we are God's children"* (Romans 8:16). When a person invites Jesus to be their Lord and Saviour and is born again, we believe their spirit is immediately made new, though not necessarily their soul or their body. The sanctifying process of discipleship and spiritual formation is what brings the body and soul into alignment with the spirit.

> *"Anyone who belongs to Christ has become a new person. The old life is gone; a new life has begun!"* (2 Corinthians 5:17 NLT)

Impure thoughts in our minds are usually not instantly erased when we turn to Christ. Emotional health is rarely granted to us immediately. An ongoing battle of the will takes place following many decisions we make; the soul takes time to be transformed. Neither is newness manifested in the physical realm immediately; our bodies take time to change and adapt. A newly born-again believer may not stop drinking excessively or doing drugs instantly. Their language may still be littered with swear words and expletives. The connection with the soul and the body needs intentional and often intensive work to be in alignment with the newness the spirit has experienced. This work of the Holy Spirit is known as sanctification. Sanctification is a lifelong process.

For a marriage to be restored fully, we need to be aware that we are **spirit** beings with a **soul** in a **body**. The diagram below may help to illustrate this concept, though of course no graphic can fully represent the mystery and intricacies of our creation.

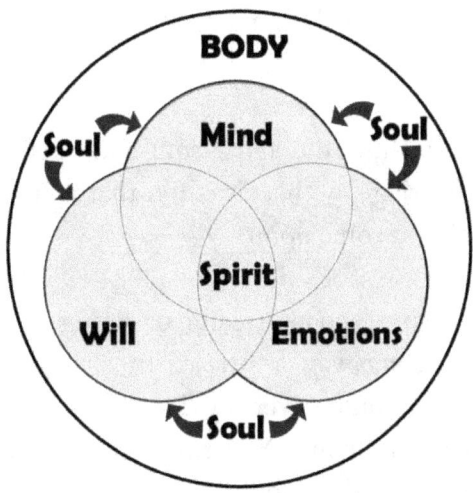

Please note that while these three realms are distinct, they are not separate entities that function independently of the others. They are intertwined and integrated. They intersect with one another. For example, when God communicates with us at the spirit level, we need our souls to receive whatever gift He has given us: Our mind helps us comprehend the revelation; sometimes we experience emotional responses such as being moved to tears or laughing. At times spiritual encounters may produce involuntary physical manifestations such as a pounding heart or trembling legs (as in Habakkuk 3:16) or falling down (as in Ezekiel 1:28 and Revelation 1:17).

We will point out these interrelated connections in more detail as we go deeper into the process of restoration. For now, let us simply say that transformation needs to take place in all three realms for your marriage to be healed in a holistic way. Addressing the hurts and trauma you may be carrying in only one or two realms may not be sufficient for lasting change.

Let us illustrate how the spirit-soul-body connection plays out in your marriage, with a situation that is likely to happen to most couples at some point.

It starts with your spouse saying or doing something that rubs you the wrong way. You react by saying something in return that Jesus would never say. They snap back with words that are equally unloving. You respond in kind once again, and soon you are in the middle of a full-blown conflict. How do you heal this rift that has developed?

To restore the peace, you could quickly say that you're sorry for what you said, for the way in which you hurt them, and offer an apology. You are sure that your apology will be accepted, and all will return to normal. This time, however, your spouse says something like, "You think an apology is going to fix this? Can't you see how hurt I am? Do you ever consider my feelings at all?" You hear them and pick up on the cue, acknowledging their feelings and thinking that will do the trick. But no luck. You have taken the soul realm into consideration, but that by itself does not always heal the rift.

Now you're wondering if you should have perhaps done something to cool down your body first. So, you go work out to let go of some steam or you go for a leisurely walk. Your spouse takes a nice, long bath. You are both feeling better physically. You're sure you've both cooled off and you offer the wounded spouse a hug or a kiss, yet they still push you away. Clearly, these attempts in the physical realm were not sufficient in themselves to bring about healing.

> We are **spirit** beings with a **soul** in a **body**... transformation needs to take place in all three realms for your marriage to be healed in a holistic way.

Now you go to prayer, asking God to forgive you and to change your spouse. You come out feeling good about what you did, only to discover that your spouse hasn't changed and is still hurt by what you said earlier. In other words, what you did in the spirit realm was not by itself enough to repair the rift either.

None of these approaches to the conflict are wrong in and of themselves. The point is, **none of them by itself brings about holistic healing that lasts**. You need to incorporate **all three realms** to heal the wound. In the example above, you may need to cool down, forgive your spouse and acknowledge the emotions aroused by the hurt. Couples in our Marriage Mentorship Process learn how to honour the spirit-soul-body connection in all aspects of married life—from conflict resolution to sex. This leads them to the point of breakthrough. Keep reading and you too will learn how.

For now, sear this concept into your brain, as we will refer to it repeatedly in the coming pages.

> We are **spirit** beings with a **soul** in a **body**…
> transformation needs to take place in all three realms
> for your marriage to be healed in a holistic way.

"MEN ARE LIKE WAFFLES, WOMEN ARE LIKE SPAGHETTI"

In this section we will make some generalizations about the ways we believe God has made men and women. These stem from our own lives as well as observations of other married couples—friends, members of the churches we have served and our mentees. Some of these generalizations may not be applicable to every couple, so you may need to reinterpret them to better fit your unique personalities. That said, we also write out of the conviction that God intentionally created men and women with innate differences that might not always be consistent but which we should not ignore.

> *"So God created human beings in his own image. In the image of God he created them; male and female he created them"* (Genesis 1:27 NLT).

In our observation, men and women are identical to each other as bearers of God's image and that's where the similarity ends! The physical differences are, of course, easy to spot. Many other differences also abound once we get past the external, visible physical realm into the soul realm.

Remember that the soul is the collective name for our mind, will and emotions. Generally speaking, men and women think and express their feelings differently. Women often express their feelings freely, while men tend to be more guarded with theirs. This may be a product of cultural conditioning, but we believe some of these differences are innate.

Most men we know tend to be more logical thinkers and problem-solvers. When his wife shares a problem with him, the husband's brain kicks into problem-solving mode. He starts spitting out possible solutions, thinking that he is being helpful. All she may have wanted him to do, however, was listen to her, acknowledge her pain and empathize with her. Bill and Pam Ferrell point out in their book, *Men Are Like Waffles, Women Are Like Spaghetti*, that women can often effortlessly move from one topic to another unrelated topic in a conversation (like spaghetti), while men tend to compartmentalize matters (as in the squares of a waffle).

These typical gender differences may not apply to you personally as a couple, but you can likely still see differences in the ways each of you respond, cope and express yourselves. Reading the Ferrells' book, answering the discussion questions for every chapter and sharing your responses will help you understand each other better and communicate more in the process.

As you learn more about yourselves, you are likely to discover how your lack of awareness of these differences may have pulled you apart and caused divisions in your marriage. For example, most wives we know long for emotional connection with their husbands before they can get excited about a sexual encounter. A husband who understands this characteristic will do everything in his power to ensure that her emotional love tank is filled to the brim. A man who is not aware of his wife's needs might resent his wife for refusing his sexual advances. He may end up accusing her of not meeting

FUNDAMENTAL PRINCIPLES

his needs: "After all I do for you and the kids, the least you could do is have sex with me."

As you begin to factor gender differences into account and make allowances for them, you will avoid much misunderstanding and heartache. In return, you will hopefully experience greater harmony and better understanding in your marriage. That is why we require all couples in our Marriage Mentorship Process to take the time to read *Men Are Like Waffles, Women Are Like Spaghetti*.[3]

> Discussion questions on the Fundamental Principles are included in the companion workbook. Get yours now at www.thesams.ca/resources or by scanning the QR code below:

---

[3] *Men Are Like Waffles, Women Are Like Spaghetti.* Bill & Pam Ferrell. Harvest House Publishers.

CHAPTER 2

ASSESSING YOUR MARRIAGE

When you go to a doctor with a persistent presenting symptom, he or she is likely to order one or more diagnostic tests. It could be a blood test, an X-ray, ultrasound, or MRI, depending on the nature of your ailment. Similarly, when you show symptoms of marital distress, you need an accurate assessment of the current state of your marriage. In our Marriage Mentorship Process, we use two different tools to assess people's relationships honestly and clearly.

ASSESSMENT #1:
THE PREPARE-ENRICH INVENTORY

Our go-to tool is a comprehensive online assessment developed by Dr. David Olson, family science pioneer, and his wife Karen Olson, in 1977. More than 4 million couples have prepared for marriage or enriched their relationships by taking the Prepare-Enrich Inventory.[4] You will discover where your marriage stands in many key areas, including Communication, Conflict Resolution, Financial Management, Leisure Activities, Sexual Relationship and Spiritual Beliefs.

To take this test, you will need a Certified Facilitator to provide you with login codes. The facilitator will also help you interpret the report. There are over 100,000 facilitators all over the world, so you should be able to find one near you on their website and take the assessment. Each of you should take the assessment separately, and your responses will be collated into a report which produces an accurate snapshot of your marriage. Your facilitator will set up a session to go through the report and may suggest action steps you can take.

Working with a facilitator is the preferred way to go, but you can also get a check-up on your own at couplecheckup.com. You will receive a report along with a guide which helps you interpret the results. Either way, this assessment is a very helpful way to start your journey from breakdown to breakthrough.

---

[4] Learn more at www.prepare-enrich.com

ASSESSMENT #2: THE LOVE LANGUAGES QUIZ

Virtually every couple seeking our marriage mentorship tells us that they still love one another. At the same time, they also admit that they are not able to experience that "love" from each other; they don't feel it. One of the reasons this paradox plays itself out repeatedly in marriages has to do with what marriage counsellor Dr. Gary Chapman calls *The Five Love Languages*.[5] To put it simply, he discovered that the way we express and experience love has a "language" of its own.

The Five Love Languages as researched by Dr. Chapman include: Words of Affirmation, Acts of Service, Receiving Gifts, Quality Time, and Physical Touch.

Each of us has one or more languages that most effectively communicate love to us. In our case, the languages that communicate love most effectively to Jeeva's heart are Acts of Service and Words of Affirmation. For Sulojana, they are Quality Time and Words of Affirmation.

When I (Jeeva) make Sulojana's breakfast every morning, wash the dishes, sweep the floor, etc., I am expressing my love for her in my default "Acts of Service" language. When she does the laundry weekly or makes the bed daily, it communicates love to me because she is speaking my language.

---

[5] www.5lovelanguages.com

As much as I (Sulojana) appreciate Jeeva doing all these chores that make my life easier, it doesn't help me sense his love all that much. However, when he makes time just for me—without his fingers glued to his cell phone—and gives me his undivided attention, then he is really speaking my language. I feel loved!

We frequently meet couples who have no idea what each other's love languages are, and this leads to frustration in their marriage. For example, a husband whose primary love language is "Words of Affirmation" heaps praise on his wife for everything she does and expects her to do the same for him. Meanwhile, her primary love language is "Physical Touch" and since he rarely touches her, she feels as though she is starved for love despite the heaping plate-full of affirming words he serves her.

What about your marriage? Do you know your spouse's primary love languages? Do you know your own? Are you "speaking" each other's languages?

Take the free quiz at 5lovelanguages.com/quizzes/couples-quiz. Once you complete the quiz, you will each receive an e-mail with a list of your love languages. Share your results with each other and see what light bulbs turn on for you. Many couples immediately begin to gain a greater understanding of how they can make things better in their marriage simply by paying attention to each other's languages of love.

To maximize the benefits of these results for your marriage, simply ask each other one key question. For example, if your

ASSESSING YOUR MARRIAGE

spouse's top love language is Physical Touch, ask them: "What kinds of physical touch make you feel loved?" Or if it is Receiving Gifts, "What kinds of gifts make you feel loved?" Make note of their responses and get to work.

For deeper study, we highly recommend you read Dr. Gary Chapman's book, *Five Love Languages*,[6] to understand each other better.

> Discussion questions on the Assessments are included in the companion workbook. Get yours now at www.thesams.ca/resources or by scanning the QR code below:

---

[6] *Five Love Languages.* Dr. Gary Chapman. Northfield Publishing.

CHAPTER 3

SHIFTING THE SPIRITUAL ATMOSPHERE

Allergy sufferers and dysfunctional married couples have one thing in common. Any idea what that is? Environmental studies have revealed repeatedly that the air inside our homes can be more toxic than the air outside. This is especially true in countries where we keep windows locked tightly, so we can enjoy the comfort of air conditioning in the summer months and heat in the winter. Add smoking, burning candles, wood-burning fireplaces, air fresheners and even cooking to the mix, and now you are breathing air that is contaminated by toxins that simply hang around. This can be the perfect breeding ground for allergies, irritation of the throat, asthma, and other lung diseases.

The young son of a couple we knew many years ago was suffering from serious allergies and asthma. His parents invested in a high-quality air cleaner from a reputable company. Within weeks, the symptoms had vanished, and he was able to function much better than before. All it took was a mechanism to remove the toxins inside their house.

Troubled couples often come to us after seeking help from external sources such as counsellors, therapists, and other specialists. They apply what they've learned and start getting results, but often find no long-term sustainability. Could it be because the atmosphere in their marriage is contaminated by pollutants such as shame, unforgiveness, ingratitude or other toxins?

The first thing we encourage couples to do once they're in the actual process itself is to clean up, purify and shift the spiritual atmosphere in their homes. Removing toxins also promotes organic growth in the marriage. There is a greenhouse effect that begins to kick in. It will make everything else that you do to achieve lasting change more effective. How do you go about doing this?

It would be great if you could simply invest in a device that could do it for you. We're sorry to disappoint you, but no such spiritual air purifier exists that we are aware of. However, you will be pleased to know that the key to shifting the spiritual atmosphere is not complicated at all. It is as simple as developing certain daily spiritual habits, and practicing them regularly, consistently, and persistently.

> *Sow a thought, reap an action; sow an action, reap a habit; sow a habit, reap a character; sow a character, reap a destiny.*
> —Ralph Waldo Emerson

Make no mistake, the habits we form will transform us, for good or for bad. But we believe that there is another significant reason why these spiritual habits are so significant. As we mentioned in our introduction, without the power of the Holy Spirit, transformation is impossible to attain and sustain. So, you as a couple, need to do all that you possibly can to ensure that the Holy Spirit is always welcome and present in your marriage. To put it another way, you don't want Him to come and visit you only when you have an expressed need. You want Him to stay with you all the time. You want Him to inhabit you individually and dwell with you collectively.

We like to say that "Spiritual habits sustain Holy Spirit habitation." These habits will help you grow in intimacy with God, and also with each other as you develop them. If these practices are new to you, add each one gradually. We have found that it takes around two weeks for most couples we mentor to incorporate all 10 habits and become consistent in practicing them.

> *Spiritual habits sustain Holy Spirit habitation.*

HABIT #1: SOAKING

In the last 20 years, meditation and mindfulness have become very popular in the West. Drawing from various Eastern traditions, much meditation emphasizes emptying your mind, sometimes by repeating a particular mantra. Contemplative prayer or what some call "Christian meditation" focuses less on emptying oneself and more on filling your entire being with the Presence of God. This is not something we can force, but something we submit to and permit to happen. As the Spirit of God fills us, things that do not belong are pushed out or brought to our attention, including negative or ungodly thoughts. We can then submit ourselves to a process of sanctification, replacing ungodly thoughts with God-thoughts from Scripture.

Many years ago, we were introduced to a form of Christian meditation called "soaking". This practice has been around in various forms for nearly 2000 years, but it was popularized in Charismatic Christian circles by John and Carol Arnott, the founding pastors of Catch The Fire church in Toronto. What we mean by "soaking" is to intentionally spend quiet time with God, allowing Him to grow your capacity for intimacy with Him. Just as you get to know your spouse by spending time with each other, so it is with God! This is His promise:

"Be still, and know that I am God" (Psalm 46:10).

When I (Jeeva) started soaking regularly, I began to experience a closeness to God that I had never experienced before. One of the practical side effects of this was that I did not get angry as easily as I used to before. This confirmed for me that soaking was a way that the Holy Spirit could change me at the core of my being. Just as baked-on grime in a pot comes off more easily when soaked in warm water for a while, some of my character flaws were worked on much more easily through soaking than when I was striving to change myself.

Soaking is a practical working out of Jesus' promise in John 15:5: *"I am the Vine; you are the branches. If you remain in me and I in you, you will bear much fruit; apart from me you can do noth-*

ing." Jesus stresses the need to simply **remain** connected to Him, as we soak in His Presence. He will then help us produce the fruit of the Spirit, which includes such Christ-like characteristics as: *"love, joy, peace, forbearance, kindness, goodness, faithfulness, gentleness and self-control"* (Galatians 5:22–23).

Carol Arnott compares soaking with the transformation of a cucumber into a dill pickle. The cucumber does nothing except to stay in the brine and get marinated. Similarly, when we place ourselves in a place of openness to the "brine" of the Holy Spirit, we are transformed. Ever since we received this revelation, we have been soaking more often, and teaching others to follow suit.

Benefits Of Soaking:

- Many discover that stress and anxiety are greatly reduced when you soak regularly.
- Most "soakers" report experiencing an overwhelming sense of God's peace.
- In that place of quiet rest, the Holy Spirit is free to do whatever He wants to do.
- You may receive healing, you may be set free from what keeps you bound, you will become more loving.
- You will be changed and become more and more like Jesus, as time progresses!

Wouldn't it be great if we could all treat our spouses as Jesus would? This is the reason we begin with soaking as the first habit you should develop and practice as a married couple to shift the spiritual atmosphere in your lives.

Musical Help?

Some people find that soft, instrumental music aids their awareness of God's Presence. This practice is found in Scripture when the prophet Elisha asked for a musician before he could receive a revelation (2 Kings 3:15). A search for "soaking instrumental music" on YouTube or your favourite music app should result in many playlists and artists available. We recommend music that is not familiar to you, so you are not distracted by singing along with it.

Some suggestions for starters (on YouTube):

>"Orchestral Soaking Music"—William Augusto
>"In His Presence"—Dappy T Keys
>"The Bliss of His Presence"—Eric Gilmour
>"While We Wait"—Nathaniel Coe III
>"The Breaking"—by Christopher Georges

Distractions And Focus

Since your brain is not used to simply doing nothing, it will start to spill out all manner of thoughts—your shopping list, your "to-do" list, your "didn't-do" list, etc. You may even see all sorts of pictures flashing across your mental screen—faces, incidents, situations, etc. Writing down all these things as they occur to you will help your mind to return to peace. Don't spend time editing or making nice lists, just get it out of your brain so you can tune into the Spirit.

After writing down your thoughts, you may still find your mind starting to wander. The best way to prevent this from happening and keep yourself on track is to focus on Jesus. You can visualize His face, as you picture Him. You can simply say His name or say: "Jesus, I love you." Or you can recite a familiar verse or passage of Scripture such as The Lord's Prayer.

This can take time and practice, so do not be discouraged if you are having difficulty quieting your mind and sensing the voice of the Spirit. If you still get any distracting thoughts, keep on writing them down. Do everything in your power to stop dwelling on them. Keep on shifting your focus to Jesus.

How Long Should You Soak?

There is no set time limit, but many find it helpful to start with a block of 10 or 15 minutes. Simply schedule it at a time that you can make it work—early morning, late evening, or any time in-between. Many people report benefits of soaking at the same time slot daily, but the main thing is that you actually make time to soak.

Write Down What You See

When you start hearing, seeing, or sensing something from God during your soaking times, write these experiences down. Don't stop to analyze your experiences, just get into the flow and stay there. Sometimes you will get only a trickle—a word or two, a picture here, a thought there. Other times it will be a torrent and you cannot write it all down fast enough. Sometimes you may alternate between long silent spaces and short bursts of revelation. All of this is normal! Just keep on writing whatever you sense.

There will also be times when it seems that nothing at all is happening, and you do not "get" anything to jot down. Do not discount the time you spend in stillness, because something is still happening when you place yourself in God's Presence. He is pouring into you what you need—wisdom, healing, love, etc. You are being transformed, whether you sense it or not. Pastors Steve & Sandra Long refer to soaking as a time of "active rest."

> *Do not discount the time you spend in stillness, because something is still happening when you place yourself in God's Presence.*

It is a bit like spending time in the sun. You don't usually feel a tan coming on! Even when you look at yourself in the mirror, you might not notice a change. But compare yourself to what you looked like a month ago and you will realize that the time you spent in the sun changed you. Similarly, you may not notice the change in yourself brought about by soaking, but those around you will, especially your spouse. There is a cumulative effect that kicks in over time. Both you and your spouse will find it easier to operate from a place of peace and rest. That will bring a tremendous difference to the way you treat one other, and your marriage will begin to experience a transformation as a result.

Initially, you will need to discipline yourself to make time to be in God's Presence every day. In time, you will ardently desire to be with the Lover of your Soul, Jesus, actually looking forward to spending as much time with Him as you possibly can.

Action Steps

1. Set aside a block of time where you are totally free from distractions. Turn off your phones. Silence all the noises that would normally bombard your senses, e.g. TV, computers, etc. If you have young children, find a time when they are safe or asleep.
2. Keep a pen and paper (preferably a notebook/journal) beside you. You may also wish to use a resource such as Carol Arnott's *Soaking Encounter Journal*.
3. Put yourself in a relaxing position. Lying down is best, in our experience. Close your eyes.
4. Say this simple prayer: "Holy Spirit, come!"
5. Stay still and wait. Do not pray or read, or do anything. Just be quiet and still.
6. If you do receive any revelations, write them down.
7. Above all, be transformed by simply being in His Presence.

HABIT #2: PRAISE AND WORSHIP

Praise and worship is another way to be transformed by the supernatural power of God's Presence. How does offering praise and worship differ from soaking? When soaking, you do nothing active, you simply place yourself in God's Presence and let the Holy Spirit change you on the inside. In praise & worship, you are actively involved. You may sing, play a musical instrument, use your body to express your emotions or any combination thereof.

According to Scripture, God is *"enthroned on the praises"* of His people (Psalm 22:3 NLT). We are also reminded that we *"enter his gates with thanksgiving and get into his courts with praise"* (Psalm 100:4 NLT). Praise gives us access to the Presence of God. When we praise God, either He comes where we are, or we go where He is.

Praise is also significant because it allows God to do for us what we cannot do for ourselves. In 2 Chronicles 20 we read how King Jehoshaphat sent a group of singers into battle at the head of the army. They started praising God with these words: *"Give thanks to the Lord, for his love endures forever."* Verses 21 & 22 describe the effect of their praise and worship upon the enemy armies. They were thrown into disarray and ended up destroying one another. Praise and worship can produce a breakthrough in the face of seemingly insurmountable obstacles.

Action Steps

> A wealth of praise and worship music can be found on YouTube or your favourite music app. Lyrics are often available online, sometimes embedded in music videos directly. Build your own playlist with songs that help you praise and worship God. You can also use CDs and DVDs if you do not have access to online resources.
>
> When you spend time soaking and then in praise and worship, you are inviting God to do for you what you cannot do on your own. You are positioning yourselves for breakthrough in your marriage. When you do it consistently, the cumulative effect results in a shift in the spiritual atmosphere of your home.

HABIT #3: GRATITUDE

In the last decade, many books have been written on the power of gratitude. You have likely heard something about this already. Scientific studies quoted in such publications as Psychology Today and Harvard Health Journal demonstrate that gratitude produces many benefits such as happiness, productivity, self-esteem, physical health, mental health, more satisfying relationships, and better sleep.[7] In our experience, gratitude is also an antidote to anxiety. A grateful spirit contributes greatly to a peaceful mind, and the peace inside of you will spill into what is outside of you, including your marriage!

---

[7] https://www.psychologytoday.com/us/basics/gratitude; https://www.health.harvard.edu/blog/in-praise-of-gratitude-201211215561

Let us look at the spiritual significance of practicing gratitude on a regular basis. As you read in the previous section: *"Enter his gates with thanksgiving and his courts with praise;* **give thanks to him and bless his holy name"** (Psalm 100:4, emphasis ours). While this is clearly an invitation to be thankful to God, we believe that the verse also implies that by expressing our gratitude to God, the doors are opened for us to enter His Presence. That is how powerful gratitude is!

Remember how we talked about spiritual habits that sustain the habitation of the Holy Spirit? Gratitude is one of these. When you enter God's Presence with thanksgiving regularly, you are less likely to react to life's events out of your basic thoughts and feelings. By practicing thankfulness, you are preparing yourself to respond to everything that happens as one who reflects God's nature and character. Might that change the way you treat your spouse? We sure think so!

Here is how you can incorporate gratitude into your daily lives.

Action Steps

Start a "Gratitude Journal" of your own or order your copy of The Unbreakable Marriage Gratitude Journal at www.thesams.ca/resources or by scanning the QR code below. Make two specific entries every day:

1. Ask yourself: **"What am I thankful for today?"** and write down your answer. You can do this either at the beginning

of the day or the end of the day. You can be thankful for things as simple as the weather, a surprise phone call or message, your home, your health, your family, the green grass, a white blanket of snow, etc. Whatever strikes you as something you can be thankful for, write it down.

2. Ask yourself: **"What is one thing about my spouse that I am thankful for today?"** and write your answer. When you are in serious conflict (as you might be right now), you may not find it easy to find something to be thankful for in the moment. If that is the case, go back to the past and come up with something from your dating days or the earlier parts of your marriage. Go as far back as you need to and write down a reason for giving thanks. Here are some basic examples to get your memory going: That time he/she made breakfast for me; when he brushed the snow off my car; when we walked hand in hand from school; that surprise gift; his/her faithfulness in taking care of the laundry, etc.

The Apostle Paul tells us to *"Give thanks in all circumstances; for this is God's will for you in Christ Jesus"* (1 Thessalonians 5:18). Your current circumstances may not seem like they are reasons for gratitude, we understand that. These are the times when you need to look past what you see in the natural and tap into the spiritual realm. *Enter into God's gates with thanksgiving!*

HABIT #4: READING THE BIBLE

The Bible is the standard by which we measure all that we teach and do in our Marriage Mentorship Process. We believe strongly that marriage is something God intended and that Holy Scripture contains much help for our marriages. Scripture is powerful to bring about breakthrough in our lives. Feeding on Holy Scripture regularly helps you develop the muscles you need to keep on ploughing forward and to endure the trials that come your way.

> *"Your word is a lamp to guide my feet and a light for my path"* (Psalm 119:105 NLT).

> *"Every Scripture has been written by the Holy Spirit, the breath of God. It will empower you by its instruction and correction, giving you the strength to take the right direction and lead you deeper into the path of godliness"* (2 Timothy 3:16 TPT).

> **God's words get into you and His Spirit lives and grows in you as seeds planted in good soil.**

To know the mind of God revealed in the words of the Bible is to know God Himself. We grow in intimacy with Him as we grow in our knowledge of what He has already revealed. We don't just read the Bible to meet some requirement of discipleship. Something genuinely incredible happens when you make Bible-reading a priority. God's words get into you and His Spirit lives and grows in you as seeds planted in good soil. Reading the Bible—along with the next two habits—will help you build your marriage on the foundation of Holy Scripture and keep reinforcing it daily. We know this sounds rather simplistic, and we know too many people have grown bored with the Bible, but it is a powerful and essential habit that needs to become part of your daily life, if it isn't already. Finding a translation that speaks your heart language and following a reading plan will help you to be consistent in reading the Bible.

For the past few years, I (Jeeva) have been following a one-year Bible reading plan, where I read the entire Bible in one year. Two such plans that have worked well for me are: The Bible in One Year with Nicky Gumbel[8] and The Daily Audio Bible with Brian Hardin.[9] Both are available as apps for your smartphone.

One thing I do is pause the recording or stop reading when a verse, phrase or word jumps out at me. I will often write it down in my journal and add any thoughts or reflections that come to me, or action steps that I need to take in response to what I read. You can also design your own plan. For example, you might read the Bible from cover to cover beginning with Genesis, or focus on the Gospels first and then the history of Israel.

My (Sulojana's) plan is to read one book of the Bible at a time. I alternate between one from the Old Testament and one from the New. I do not set a goal of how many verses or chapters

---

[8] Available from bible.com/reading-plans/17704-bible-in-one-year-2020-with-nicky-gumbel

[9] Available from dailyaudiobible.com

to read every day. I read as many as I can, taking the time to pause and reflect, making notes on revelations I receive.

Regardless of how you choose to do it, please make sure you read the Bible every day. We would highly recommend that you do it in a systematic, structured way as suggested. Just opening the Bible to a random page and reading what is on that page is not something we encourage. Yes, there will be times when the first passage that catches your eyes is highly relevant for that moment. But you are not likely to capture the entire arc of God's story this way. You could be depriving yourself of the wisdom and beauty of God's work with His beloved children if you do not read the entire Bible.

Action Step

What is your Bible reading plan? _____

HABIT #5: LISTENING TO SCRIPTURE

We have discovered that the power of Scripture is compounded when we hear it read aloud, either in our own voice or by another. This is why we created an audio recording of Scriptures pertaining to marriage, read by us, with quiet soaking music in the background, produced by our son, Sathiya, who is a musician. Many couples whom we have mentored have discovered the power of allowing these Scriptures to enter into their being on a daily basis. Whether you listen to us, read the Bible aloud to yourself, or listen to someone else do so, we believe you will encounter God afresh.

Action Step

> Download this recording at www.thesams.ca/resources (or scan the QR code below) and listen to it at least once a day.

HABIT #6: SHARING SPIRITUAL INSIGHTS

The third Scripture-based habit you need to develop is sharing spiritual insights with one another daily. Does that sound scary? Fear not, it is really a simple task. You have already laid the groundwork for it by reading, listening and contemplating Scripture. We're suggesting now that you share your thoughts. Whether you received pictures, action steps, or simply things that came to mind that you wrote down, share these with your spouse.

You might also take one extra step that we have been taking for a few years now. Both of us have subscribed to the same daily devotionals that get delivered by e-mail. They are usually waiting for us as we begin the day. We read them on our own and share any insights that jumped out at us from those devotionals. Personally, we have been blessed by Kenneth and Gloria Copeland's "Faith to Faith Daily," Joyce Meyer's "Promises for Everyday Life," Os Hillman's

"Today God Is First", "The Upper Room," and "Our Daily Bread" to name a few. Print resources work just as well. The purpose of this time of sharing spiritual insights is for you to communicate with each other every day at a deep spiritual level.

Not surprisingly, this time of sharing has led us to take some significant action steps in obedience to the Holy Spirit. One day my (Jeeva's) readings included references to how God is deeply concerned about the poor, widows and orphans (i.e. those who cannot help themselves, through no fault of their own). This led us to seek out and support ministries that specialized in helping orphans, widows, and the poor.

Similarly, as I (Sulojana) was reading the familiar account of Jesus breaking bread with His disciples, what the church now celebrates as the Eucharist, or the Lord's Supper, I was stopped in my tracks by the words: *"For as often as you eat this bread and drink this cup, you proclaim the Lord's death till He comes"* (1 Corinthians 11:26 NKJV). Especially the words *"as often as"* jumped out at me. We had both already heard of people who celebrated the Lord's Supper at least once a day and sometimes even more frequently, but we had never acted on it ourselves. That day, those words *"as often as"* prompted us to ask, "How often is that for us?" We decided right then and there that we would end every day by reading 1 Corinthians 11:23–26 and sharing the Lord's Supper together.[10]

---

[10] We realize that the practice of daily communion or celebrating the Eucharist at home is not encouraged by all churches. Our intent in sharing this is not to offend anyone, but simply to include an example of sharing spiritual insights that can change your life in concrete ways.

HABIT #7: PRAYING IN AGREEMENT

"Truly I tell you that if two of you on earth agree about anything they ask for, it will be done for them by my Father in heaven" (Matthew 18:19).

What a remarkable promise Jesus makes in these words! It only takes two to come into agreement, and when that happens, God moves. In a marriage, the "two" is a wife and a husband. We have made it a point to pray together at the end of every day, but you can do it at any other time of the day that works for you. If the prospect of praying out aloud together is intimidating for you, try following this simple pattern that we use.

Thanksgiving

Begin by thanking God for all your blessings and for each other. This is in keeping with what God asks us to do: *"Do not be anxious about anything, but in every situation, by prayer and petition, with thanksgiving, present your requests to God"* (Philippians 4:6).

If you have already noted down some things to be thankful for in your gratitude journal, then this will be an easy step. Just read out loud what you wrote in response to Question #1: "What am I thankful for today?" and add other reasons for thanksgiving, for example:

"I thank you, God, for the walk we took together today."
"I thank you, God, for the great meal my husband cooked for us."

"I thank you, God, for the sale my wife made in her business."

Requests

Next, bring your prayer requests to God. Begin with the needs of others you are aware of—family, friends, those in your community, those affected by painful events (local, national and global). We keep a prayer journal where we list those who have requested prayer from us or those for whom we sense a burden and pray for them.

Then bring your own needs—your health, spiritual life, emotions, finances, job or business, to God. This ordering is not magical, but it is a way to model Jesus who always put others before himself.

Receive

After we have prayed for these needs, we hold our hands together, lift them up to the heavens and pull them down as a symbolic way of receiving the answers to our prayers from God. This is in accordance with what Jesus taught in Mark 11:24: *"Therefore, I tell you, whatever you ask for in prayer, believe that you **have received** it, and it will be yours."* (emphasis ours)

Seal

Finally, we seal all our prayers in the name of Jesus, by repeating together the prayer Jesus taught His disciples in

Matthew 6:9–13. Here is our slightly modified King James Version of The Lord's Prayer:

> *Our Father who art in heaven,*
> *Hallowed be Thy name.*
> *Thy kingdom come,*
> *Thy will be done,*
> *On earth as it is in heaven.*
> *Give us this day our daily bread.*
> *And forgive us our trespasses,*
> *as we forgive those who trespass against us.*
> *And lead us not into temptation, but deliver us from evil:*
> *For Thine is the kingdom, and the power, and the glory, for ever and ever. Amen.*

This is the framework we use; it has been helpful for us, but please do not feel any pressure to follow it. The power of praying together is not in the format you follow or the exact words you use. It lies in the power of agreement that Jesus has promised us. We have seen many prayers answered in miraculous ways when we came into agreement with each other—relationships restored, financial breakthroughs and healings, to name just a few.

> **The power of praying together is not in the format you follow or the exact words you use. It lies in the power of agreement that Jesus has promised us.**

One final word: if business travel or military service or anything else separates you from one another physically, don't let that stop you from praying together. Use the phone, video chat or whatever other mechanism works for you, as much as is humanly possible. The power of praying in agreement is explosive. Don't miss out on it!

Action Steps

1. Write down some reasons for thanksgiving that you would include in prayer today.
2. Write down requests on your hearts.
   a. Needs of others _____
   b. Your personal needs _____
3. Write down the declarations you are making and symbolically pull them down from heaven.
4. Seal them with the Lord's Prayer.

HABIT #8: REFRAINING FROM THE 4 C's

Shifting the spiritual atmosphere requires you to add certain positive elements to your daily life, such as the habits of soaking, gratitude and sharing spiritual insights. It also requires you to remove certain negative elements from your life, which we call the "4 C's".

The origin of the "4 C's" dates back to the season of Lent on the Christian calendar in 2010. We were preparing to observe a 40-day fast in our church. I (Jeeva) was reading through Isaiah 58, a section of Scripture devoted to fasting. God was sharing in that passage what kind of fast was pleasing to Him and what was not acceptable. God was displeased with people who observed ritual fasts but continued to engage in ungodly behaviours such as picking fights and quarrels, not taking care of their family, ignoring the poor and oppressing the helpless.

Tucked in the midst of this list was a reference in verse 9 to *"the pointing finger and malicious talk."* Those two items stopped me cold in my tracks. I realized that while I was doing fairly well on the spiritual scoreboard, I was guilty of these two offences. As I started reflecting on what fasting from "the pointing finger and malicious talk" meant for me in practical terms, I remembered a quote from Dale Carnegie, "Never criticize, condemn or complain...any fool can, and most fools do."[11]

Ouch! Whenever I criticized or condemned others, I was pointing the finger at them, not realizing that there were three fingers pointing back at me. When I engaged in this kind of behaviour, I was guilty of malicious talk too.

---

[11] *How to Win Friends and Influence People*, Dale Carnegie, Gallery Books

One of my mentors from an earlier period in my life called them the 3 C's. The Holy Spirit showed me a fourth C that many of us are guilty of: comparing! I was comparing myself to others and either feeling good because they were not doing as well as I was, or feeling bad because I was not doing as well as they were. Once again you can see that this qualified on both counts, *"the pointing finger and malicious talk."*

> Observe a fast of the "4 C's"—Criticizing, Complaining, Condemning and Comparing.

That Lenten season, Sulojana and I challenged ourselves and our church to observe a fast of the "4 C's"—Criticizing, Complaining, Condemning and Comparing. It sounded easy to do but in reality, it was anything but. As a matter of fact, many of our folks told us that they would have preferred to give up another set of 4 C's: chocolate, cookies, chips and cakes! Yet, when we persisted in refraining from criticizing, complaining, condemning and comparing, the blessings and breakthroughs we received were simply confounding! We discovered that fasting from the "4 C's" caused a shift in the spiritual atmosphere of our homes and our church!

If you start practising this habit, we believe you will realize this shift in the spiritual atmosphere of your marriage as well.

Action Steps

1. Decide to start refraining from the "4 C's" right away.

2. Give your spouse permission to catch you in the act of criticizing, complaining, condemning, and comparing. We have a lot of fun with it. Whenever one person slips up, the other person simply says with a smile: "4 C's!"

3. For an added incentive, throw a dollar (or more) in a jar every time you violate one of the "4 C's". Treat yourself to something you enjoy with the loot you accumulate or give away the money to a charity of your choice at the end of the week.

Do not be discouraged if you have some big fails when you first get started on this. Old habits die hard. The good news is that they do eventually die if you keep on starving them. Give yourself a pass, even when you fail to catch yourself in time before one of the C's slips off your tongue! Becoming aware of them is the starting point. Doing your best to avoid them will eventually contribute to breakthrough.

HABIT #9: BLESSING YOUR SPIRIT

This daily habit is particularly powerful, yet not many people are aware of it. We have drawn from the teaching of Arthur Burk—founder of the Sapphire Leadership Group, a Christian think-tank—who has graciously given his blessing to what we are writing in this section.

Arthur was aware of how we can influence our souls (mind, will and emotions) with our words. He wondered whether we could do the same with our spirit. At that time, most ministry methods were not taking into consideration the distinction between the spirit and the soul, such as we find in Hebrews 4:12. He was also struck by the words of the blessing found in 1 Thessalonians 5:23 NLT (which we mentioned earlier):

> *"May God Himself, the God of peace, sanctify you through and through. May your whole **spirit, soul and body** be kept blameless at the coming of our Lord Jesus Christ."*

Notice how the blessing begins with the spirit, then the soul and finally the body.

He started to share this revelation about blessing one's spirit with others, who then applied it to various situations. We have heard anecdotal reports of parents who started blessing the spirits of their babies in the womb during pregnancy. When some of these babies were in the breach position and the parents commanded their spirits to move in alignment with God's plans, they "turned themselves" into the proper position (without any external intervention) and were delivered by natural birth.

We also heard about a mother with an autistic son. She could not get through to his soul with her words, so she started blessing his spirit. After several years, the son was declared healed of autism. Wow! There are also testimonies of parents blessing the spirits of their prodigal children and seeing them come back to the Lord!

Several years ago, at a Love After Marriage Workshop, we heard Barry and Lori Byrne, founders of Nothing Hidden Ministries, share how blessing each other's spirits had transformed couples whose marriages were in distress. That is when we began developing the habit of blessing each other's spirits ourselves. After a few weeks, Jeeva noticed that he could not get mad at Sulojana for anything, even if he wanted to! Since incorporating this daily spiritual habit into our Marriage Mentorship Process, we have been receiving good reports from the couples we have mentored as well.

Action Steps

> Here is how you bless each other's spirit, as a couple:
>
> 1. Look each other in the eye for 30 seconds straight. This might seem like an eternity when you first try it, but it gets easier. (You're allowed to blink, by the way!)
> 2. For the **morning**, offer this blessing: "_____ (name), I bless your spirit to rise up and walk hand in hand with Holy Spirit all through the day."
>
>   For the **evening**: "_____ (name), I bless your spirit to receive all that Holy Spirit releases to you all through the night."

That's it. It's really that simple. There are times when you may need to improvise the way you do the blessing, especially when you are not together physically to look into each other's eyes. You can bless each other over the phone, through video chat, or even via text message! It is still just as powerful. We hope it is effective for you too and we look forward to hearing your testimonies.

HABIT #10: MAKING DECLARATIONS

"She is always late!"
"He is never home!"

Have you ever had such thoughts? Or worse, spoken them? Chances are that she still continues to be late for everything, and he is seldom home. Your complaining words were also a declaration that affected their ongoing behaviour, whether you realized it or not. Here are two passages of scripture that alert us to this reality:

> *"You will also declare a thing, and it will be established for you…"* (Job 22:28 NKJV).

> *"For assuredly, I say to you, whoever says to this mountain, 'Be removed and be cast into the sea,' and does not doubt in his heart, but believes that those things he says will be done, he will have whatever he says"* (Mark 11:23 NKJV).

Jesus is illustrating here a powerful reality with a dramatically vivid image. You can call things forth to life which do not exist right now as though they did. While God can create new realities in our lives directly, He invites us to co-create with Him by the way we speak about ourselves and our lives. Consider this striking illustration in the Bible.

Abraham And Sarah's Declarations

Abraham had faith in God, *"who gives life to the dead and calls those things which do not exist as though they did"* (Romans 4:17 NJKV). God brings things into existence and gives life to the dead with His words. We who are created in the image of God can also do the same. Interestingly, Abraham and Sarah did this by simply saying their own names out loud.

In Genesis 17, God changed their names from Abram to Abraham and Sarai to Sarah. Abram means "exalted father." Abraham means "father of a multitude/many nations." Sarai means "princess." Sarah means "noblewoman, mother of many nations." So, whenever Abram said: "I am Abraham," he was making the declaration: "I am the father of many nations." Similarly, whenever Sarai said, "I am Sarah," she was declaring: "I am the mother of many nations." Whenever they addressed each other by their new names, they were declaring that each other would be—and already were, prophetically—the father and mother of many nations.

To appreciate the irony of that, remember that at the time of this name change, Abraham was 99 and Sarah was 89 years old. She had been certified barren by the obstetricians and gynecologists of her day. Yet, within a year of the name change and making these declarations, they had become parents of a

> *You can call things forth to life which do not exist right now as though they did.*

bouncing baby boy named Isaac. This happened despite the fact that both of them laughed in unbelief when their names were changed by God! God performed a miracle in Sarah's body and He invited Abraham and Sarah's participation in declaring what He would do through them. Life was indeed in the power of the tongue! (Proverbs 18:21)

Action Steps

Take this familiar passage. Chances are you have heard these verses read at weddings, perhaps even your own!

> *"Love is patient, love is kind. It does not envy, it does not boast, it is not proud. It does not dishonour others, it is not self-seeking, it is not easily angered, it keeps no record of wrongs. Love does not delight in evil but rejoices with the truth. It always protects, always trusts, always hopes, always perseveres. Love never fails"* (1 Corinthians 13:4–8a).

The apostle Paul is listing a series of attributes of God's kind of love that we can manifest in our lives, including our marriages. Here's how you can harness the power of making declarations to create a breakthrough:

1. Make a declaration about yourself: *"I am patient, I am kind. I do not envy, I do not boast, I am not proud. I do not dishonour others, I am not self-seeking, I am not easily angered, I keep no record of wrongs. I do not delight in*

> *evil but rejoice with the truth. I always protect, always trust, always hope, always persevere. My love never fails."*

You may feel uneasy saying things about yourself that you know are not true right now. That is exactly how Sarah and Abraham must have felt, declaring each other as the mother and father of many nations when they had not even made one baby together! Nonetheless, God invited them to speak the future into the present, and they did not allow their misgivings to keep them from obedience. We are not asking you to lie to yourself (or anyone else), but rather to speak out a new reality, one that is already real in Christ, and is becoming real for you each day as you are sanctified.

2. Make a declaration about your spouse. Substitute their first name in the blanks and read this aloud: *"_____ is patient, _____ is kind. _____ does not envy, does not boast, is not proud. _____ does not dishonour others and is not self-seeking. _____ is not easily angered and keeps no record of wrongs. _____ does not delight in evil but rejoices with the truth. _____ always protects, always trusts, always hopes, always perseveres. _____'s love never fails."*

As you read these words out loud, you might very well hear a voice screaming inside your head, "That is not true, and you know it!" Recognize that this voice is only stating the facts and press on to declare the truth of what God says is possible for you anyway.

Time and again we have seen couples in our Marriage Mentorship Process make these declarations about themselves and each other, even though they may feel phony. With time, they begin to see the changes in themselves and each other. They discover that the Scripture *"You will have whatever you say"* is true after all! We believe the same will be true for you.

DAILY HABITS PRODUCE LIFELONG RESULTS

You may have heard that practicing a habit for 21 days in a row helps ensure that it becomes a permanent part of your life. Neuroscientists say that a new neural pathway is made in your physical brain when you keep on practicing a habit repeatedly. Dr. Caroline Leaf takes it one step further in her book *Switch on Your Brain*,[12] teaching that when you repeat that 21-day period for two more cycles (a total of 63 days), that habit will become a permanent part of your being. Thus, in our Marriage Mentorship Process, we allow couples two weeks to learn these spiritual habits and start applying them. Then we expect them to be consistent with all of them, every day, for 63 days in a row, without fail. We know this is asking a lot, but we believe in the results. Is your marriage worth it?

At the time of writing, every couple who has received our mentorship and maintained this consistency has achieved

---

[12] *Switch On Your Brain*. Dr. Caroline Leaf. p. 152

their breakthrough, without exception. More importantly, most of them report that they continue to practice these habits long after they complete their mentorship with us.

One simple way to stay on track is to use a spreadsheet. For couples in our Marriage Mentorship Process, we set it up online so we can monitor how consistent they are. You can just as easily set up an offline spreadsheet, print it out and check off the boxes manually. Or use the template in the workbook.

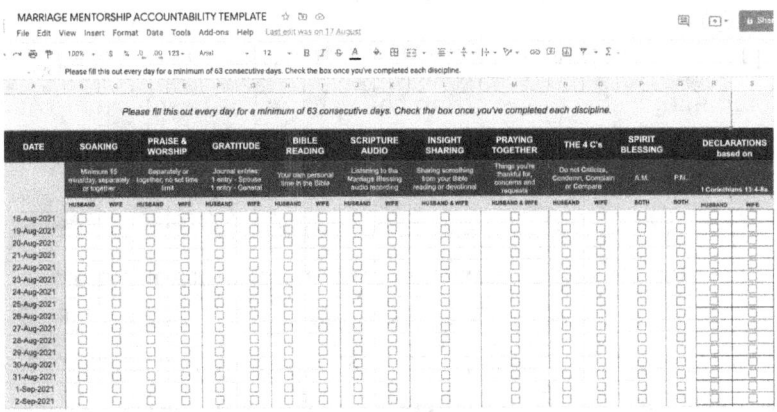

Regardless of how you choose to track it, you will see the most effective and lasting change by setting up some form of accountability. Choose an accountability partner, a mentoring couple, or someone other than your spouse who will "hold your feet to the fire" and help you stay on track. This is one of the keys to producing breakthrough in your marriage. Without taking this step of accountability, you are much less likely to experience the kind of results couples have experienced by following this process.

Action Steps

1. Set up your Accountability Sheet. Feel free to use the one we have provided in The Unbreakable Marriage Workbook at www.thesams.ca/resources.

2. Who are some couples or individuals you can ask to be your Accountability Partners?

HOW TO SHIFT THE SPIRITUAL ATMOSPHERE SWIFTLY

The daily habits you have started to develop will have a cumulative effect on shifting the spiritual atmosphere in your home. But there are times when you need to shift the atmosphere in a hurry.

One night, a couple we were mentoring got into an argument. It began to escalate. Verbal missiles went back and forth, inflicting further damage. By this time, they had at their disposal some tools they could have used to defuse the crisis (you will learn them in Chapter 6). But they were unable or unwilling to use them in the heat of the moment.

In that moment of utter desperation, they remembered that they had 24/7 access to us for the duration of their mentorship. They sent us a text and we called them right back, despite the late hour. Very clearly, they had hit the proverbial wall and we needed to break the impasse right then and there.

We asked them to say these three words out aloud: "HOLY SPIRIT, COME!" Then we asked them to pause and remain still for a couple of minutes. What happened next was nothing short of miraculous. This couple, who were ripping each other to shreds mere moments ago, calmed down almost instantly. Within minutes they were able to apply the tools and move towards a place of peace and restoration.

What Changed?

Let's analyze what happened. Firstly, they reached out for help rather than prolong the misery on their own. This broke some of the tension in the air and allowed the burden to be carried by more people. Secondly, once they heard our counsel and took it, making intentional room for the Spirit of God to come and interrupt things, there was a shift in the spiritual atmosphere around them.

> *You ask for the Holy Spirit; you get the Holy Spirit. Just like that!*

Are you surprised that it happened so swiftly? You shouldn't be! After all, this is exactly what is supposed to happen, according to Jesus:

> *"If you then, though you are evil, know how to give good gifts to your children, how much more will your Father in heaven give the Holy Spirit to those who ask him!"* (Luke 11:13)

Notice that there are no conditions attached to this promise. You ask for the Holy Spirit; you get the Holy Spirit. Just like that! No wonder something happened swiftly when this couple said: "Holy Spirit, come!" He came, and He shifted the spiritual atmosphere. They received the power to break their impasse, and while they still had to work on the issue that caused the conflict, they did not make a bad situation any worse.

Whenever you hit a stalemate like this couple did, invite God to come and disrupt the situation. Simply cry out: "Holy Spirit, come!" and then wait upon His Presence. You will be amazed at how swiftly the spiritual atmosphere shifts and paves the way for the hard work of reconciliation to begin!

> Discussion questions on this chapter are included in the companion workbook. Get yours now at www.thesams.ca/resources or by scanning the QR code below:

CHAPTER 4

REMOVING SPIRITUAL BLOCKAGES

THE REAL ENEMY

Congratulations on taking the steps to shifting the spiritual atmosphere in your marriage! As you are adding these habits, you also need to be aware of blockages in the spirit realm that can stand in the way of receiving your breakthrough. We will now shift our attention to identifying and removing these spiritual blockages. To begin this process, we must identify who the real enemy is behind all your hardship.

When you have an argument or a full-blown fight in your marriage, it often feels as though you are in a boxing match. One person throws a punch. The other one hits back. One jabs harder. You return the favour. The conflict escalates. Words get harsher, the fight gets nastier. Low blows. Upper cuts. You don't care, you are going to win this fight, one way or the other.

You begin to treat each other as enemies in the natural, as those who are deliberately trying to make life miserable for you. If you look at what is happening in the spirit realm, however, you will realize that your spouse is not the real enemy you are fighting. The apostle Paul reminds us:

> *"For our struggle is not against flesh and blood, but against the rulers, against the authorities, against the powers of this dark world and against the spiritual forces of evil in the heavenly realms"* (Ephesians 6:12).

> **While you fight each other as though you were enemies, the Real Enemy is standing there watching and clapping his hands in glee!!**

While you fight each other as though you were enemies, the Real Enemy is standing there watching and clapping his hands in glee!! In this scenario, it is never you or your spouse who wins, but Satan. Everyone else loses.

This is why we encourage all couples to determine never to look at their spouse as the enemy. Satan is the real enemy, his name literally means "Adversary" or "Accuser." He is on a mission *"to steal and kill and destroy"* (John 10:10). Are you going to let him destroy your marriage? We certainly hope not.

The good news is that we know exactly how to win this battle. The apostle Paul reminds us: *"...Satan will not outsmart us. For we are familiar with his evil schemes"* (2 Corinthians 2:11 NLT). Also, *"For though we walk in the flesh, we do not war according to the flesh. For the weapons of our warfare are not carnal but mighty in God for pulling down strongholds..."* (2 Corinthians 10:3–4 NKJV).

You cannot win a spiritual battle with physical weapons. Spiritual battles call for spiritual weapons and spiritual strategies.

TAKING THOUGHTS CAPTIVE

The first strategy we use to prevent arguments from escalating into battles is this: *"...bringing every thought into captivity to the obedience of Christ"* (2 Corinthians 10:5 NKJV).

Take this simple thought as an example: "He always ignores me." That thought by itself might not do any damage, but when you dwell on it and agree with it, you start taking offense and before you know it, you will act out in response to it. You get into an angry argument or dirty fight or simply fume in silence. You can avoid all this trouble by intentionally recognizing the thought, calling it out and taking it captive. How do you do this practically?

You begin by first shifting the spiritual atmosphere. Remember those three powerful words? Say them now: "Holy Spirit, come!" Next you use this simple tool.

The H.A.L.T. Method

Picture yourself as a police officer. Police officers must be obeyed because they have both power and authority. The power can be brute physical force, a baton or a firearm. Their authority is delegated to them by their city, region or nation, via the rule of law and identified by their badge. They are given permission to use violence to enforce their authority.

Similarly, you have power that comes from the Holy Spirit (Acts 1:8). You carry authority that was delegated to you by Jesus *"over all the power of the enemy"* (Luke 10:19 NKJV). All you need to do now is to exercise that authority and use that power to take thoughts captive.

This is what H.A.L.T stands for:

> **H**old that thought!
> **A**rrest that thought.
> **L**ock it up in a cell with Jesus.
> **T**hank Jesus for taking care of that thought.

Let's apply the H.A.L.T. method to a thought some men might have, such as, "She always nags me." Say out loud:

> HOLD! Thought about my wife nagging me, hold it!
> ARREST! "She's always nagging me," you're under arrest.
> LOCK! Thought, I'm locking you up in a cell with Jesus.
> THANK! Thank you, Jesus, for taking care of this thought.

Despite how simple this appears to be, we and countless others have found it to be very effective. God has given us authority over our souls, which includes our own thoughts. You can pay attention to the contents of your mind and H.A.L.T. anything that does not agree with Jesus.

FORGIVING OTHERS

The second strategy we use is found in these words of the apostle Paul: *"I also forgive…lest Satan should take advantage of us"* (2 Corinthians 2:10–11 NKJV). In other words, we give Satan room to delay and even prevent our breakthrough when we choose not to forgive those who have wronged us. Here is what Jesus himself has to say:

> *"Therefore, if you are offering your gift at the altar and there remember that your brother or sister has something against you, leave your gift there in front of the altar. First go and be reconciled to them; then come and offer your gift"* (Matthew 5:23–24).

Jesus values forgiveness so much that he tells us to go take care of any unforgiveness we may have before we even engage in worship! That's something to think about.

By the way, when we talk about forgiving others, we are not talking about the hurts caused by your spouse alone. While you will likely have plenty to deal with regarding your spouse, chances are good that you have been hurt by others. If you have never audited the pain in your life, it is worth taking some time to reflect on offenses you may be holding on to, all the way back to your childhood. Unforgiveness towards any person that has hurt you can potentially block your breakthrough. It is wise to do everything in our power to remove the hold that people have over us, by forgiving them all.

Unfortunately, there are some serious misunderstandings about what forgiveness is and what it is not. Let us clear them up first before we get into the nitty gritty of practicing forgiveness.

Forgiveness Is Not…

…reconciliation. Forgiving someone does not mean that we are automatically reconciled with them or that our relationship is back to "normal." Forgiveness takes only one to offer, but reconciliation takes two to work out over time. We can forgive someone on our own, but the one being forgiven, the one who wronged us, needs to acknowledge the hurt they caused and the effects of that hurt upon us before reconciliation is even possible.

…forgetting what happened. To forgive does not mean that we forget the hurt or behave as though it never happened. We should never minimize the wounds caused by the hurt. Paradoxically, however, as we release forgiveness and receive healing for our hurt, we can eventually get to a place where the sting of prior hurt is reduced, when we remember it. Even though we may still sport scars, the power of that hurt to control us can be diminished and even eliminated, by God's grace.

...erasing responsibility. When we forgive, we are not absolving the offender of their responsibility in causing the hurt. They are not off the hook for what they did. What they did was not right. However, we do not take responsibility for punishing them or exacting revenge upon them. As Paul reminds us: *"Dear friends, never take revenge. Leave that to the righteous anger of God. For the Scriptures say, 'I will take revenge; I will pay them back,' says the Lord"* (Romans 12:10, NLT).

...tolerating ongoing hurt. If someone keeps on hurting us, we should remove ourselves from harm's way even after we forgive them. Forgiveness does not replace your need for safety. We can *"speak the truth in love"* (Ephesians 4:15a) to the offender and ask them to stop their hurtful words or actions. We need to set boundaries as to what is acceptable and what is not. When those boundaries keep on getting violated, we should report the hurt and/or the abuse to the authorities, where appropriate, for the sake of ourselves as well as the wider community.

...restoring trust. We may choose to forgive a spouse who has done something to break the trust in the marriage (not honouring confidentiality, spending recklessly, committing adultery, nursing a secret addiction, etc.), but this does not automatically result in trust being restored. Forgiveness is given freely, but trust must be earned—one step at a time, over time.

Forgiveness is an important part of healing, but it does not change your wider situation on its own. If there are major issues of trust, safety, etc. they must be dealt with! Forgiveness does not excuse what has been done to you, but it is a part of your journey towards a fuller life.

Unforgiveness, on the other hand, can keep you from a breakthrough, as this passage implies:

> **Forgiveness is given freely, but trust must be earned—one step at a time, over time.**

"Truly I tell you, if anyone says to this mountain, 'Go, throw yourself into the sea,' and does not doubt in their heart but believes that what they say will happen, it will be done for them. Therefore, I tell you, whatever you ask for in prayer, believe that you have received it, and it will be yours. And when you stand praying, if you hold anything against anyone, forgive them, so that your Father in heaven may forgive you your sins" (Mark 11:23–25).

If you have only ever heard this passage used to teach about miraculous faith, then it may seem strange that Jesus would follow it up with a teaching on forgiveness. It seems that Jesus is saying that if you have any offense that you haven't released through forgiveness, you'd better take care of it. Otherwise, it could prevent you from receiving the breakthrough you are believing for.

Forgiveness Is...

...a decision. Forgiveness is not an emotion or a feeling. To forgive, we need to make a decision to offer it as a deliberate act of the will. We do not wait till we feel like forgiving. We simply choose to cancel the debt. We also do not wait for the person who hurt us to apologize or express remorse first. That apology may never come, but we can use our power and authority to choose to forgive and be free.

...a process. Even though the decision to forgive may be made in an instant, it often marks the beginning of a journey where we process the effects of that hurt upon us and receive the healing we need in our soul and even in our body. This takes time, and we must not rush the process or be rushed into it, thinking we can get it over and done with. Forgiveness can often be like peeling off the layers of an onion. Even when reconciliation does not seem possible, we continue working through our own forgiveness, for our sake, and in obedience to God.

...an unconditional act. Ultimately, the forgiveness we offer others is in response to the forgiveness we have received from God Himself. Since God does not impose any conditions upon us before He will forgive us, neither do we. We can never say, "I'll forgive you *if/when* you do these things," for that is not forgiveness. We forgive with no strings attached so that our forgiveness reflects the forgiveness we have received from God.

…a command. Scripture is clear that forgiveness is a way of life if you are to follow Jesus. Since receiving God's free gift of forgiveness is the beginning of our new life in Christ, it is not optional for us to release it. *"Forgive as the Lord forgave you"* (Colossians 3:13b); *"And forgive us our debts, as we also have forgiven our debtors"* (Matthew 6:12). Forgiveness is very simply something Christians must do when someone sins against them.

…a response from the heart. Jesus makes this clear in the parable of the unforgiving servant, where the main character is an employee who had been forgiven a huge debt. When he refused to forgive one who owed him a much smaller amount, the master who forgave his huge debt handed him over to the jailers to be tortured, until he should pay back all he owed. Jesus goes on to warn, *"This is how my heavenly Father will treat each of you unless you forgive your brother or sister from your heart"* (Matthew 18:35). He says that forgiving honestly will keep us from being *"handed over to the torturers"* (v. 34). In other words, the enemy has permission to keep on haunting and torturing us, unless we also *"forgive from the heart."*

Forgiving From The Heart

To grasp the significance of what Jesus meant by this expression, it is helpful to consider what the word "heart" used in Scripture describes.

1. The physical organ. *"A sound heart is the life of the flesh"* (Proverbs 14:30).

2. The mind, the place where thoughts originate. *"For it is from within, out of a person's heart, that evil thoughts come"* (Mark 7:21).
3. The seat of emotions. *"A cheerful heart is good medicine"* (Proverbs 17:22). *"The Lord regretted that he had made human beings on the earth, and his heart was deeply troubled"* (Genesis 6:6).
4. The place where the will is exercised. *"If you are returning to the Lord with all your hearts, then rid yourselves of the foreign gods…and commit yourselves to the Lord and serve him only…"* (1 Samuel 7:3).

As you can see, what we call the soul is included in what the Bible calls the heart. It is a loaded word which describes the condition of our inner being manifested in our outer being, often in our words. To paraphrase Jesus in Luke 6:45: *"The mouth speaks what the heart is full of."* It is also true of our actions, as Proverbs 4:23 reminds us: *"Above all else, guard your heart, for everything you do flows from it."*

> **Forgiving from the heart takes seriously the effects of a person's hurt upon our entire being.**

While we cannot be entirely certain what Jesus' exact intended meaning was, it is clear from experience that forgiving *from the heart* takes seriously the effects of a person's hurt upon our entire being, which includes the mind, will, and emotions, even the body itself.

Traumatic events (such as a breakup, betrayal, adultery, physical abuse, sexual assault, violent attack, abandonment, accidents, etc.) are recorded in the body, as author Bessel van der Kolk demonstrates vividly in *The Body Keeps The Score*. Effects upon the body can include being triggered by certain sounds or smells, becoming immobilized, experiencing changes in heart rates and/or blood pressure, becoming dependent on medications, drugs, alcohol, or other addictive substances, cutting oneself and loss of sleep, to name just a few.

Effects upon the soul often include anxiety, depression, flashbacks, feeling unsafe, nightmares, fits of rage, emotional shutdowns, etc. Another of the effects on the soul is how the enemy tempts us to believe certain lies that we might never believe otherwise. We are especially vulnerable to these distortions when we experience trauma or repeated hurts inflicted by the same person, especially parents, siblings, a teacher, a pastor, a boss, a co-worker, or your spouse.

Take for example, a woman who experiences an unforeseen breakup with her partner. In this time of hurt, the enemy whispers, "See how he broke up with you just like that? It's because you're not loveable. You're not attractive. You're incapable of making a relationship last. You'll always be stuck here. Men can't be trusted anyway; they'll woo you, use you and then drop you."

Under normal circumstances, this woman might have identified these as obvious lies and told the enemy to take a hike. In a wounded state, however, she is vulnerable and more likely to agree with those lies. This often leads to ungodly responses such as hatred, mistrust, shame, fear, self-hatred, unforgiveness, bitterness and rage, to name a few. She may even go on to make inner vows such as, "I'll never trust a man again," or "Why ever bother to even get into another relationship?"

Or consider a young man who has heard his father say repeatedly, "You will not amount to anything good." He grows up believing that he is worthless and will not be successful at anything he does. He might make inner vows too, in response: "I won't reach too high. I will settle for whatever I can find."

Repeated hurts and trauma continue to affect a person's ability to be and become all that God created them to be. When you come into a marriage with unhealed hurts, you will relate to each other from a place of hurt and end up hurting each other even more. Forgiveness does not stop the outside world from hurting you, but it is a powerful tool to restrict the extent of the harm on the inside. This is why we strongly urge to you take the time and be patient as you practice forgiveness from your heart. Attempting to rush this process will not help.

> **When you come into a marriage with unhealed hurts, you will relate to each other from a place of hurt and end up hurting each other even more.**

Action Steps

Ask the Holy Spirit: "Who do I need to forgive? What injustices have been done to me that I am still holding on to?"

Chances are high that your spouse will make the list, along with others close to you, such as your parents, siblings, other family members and friends, former boyfriends or girlfriends, co-workers, bosses, teachers, and anyone else who betrayed you or hurt you in the past. Write down every name without questioning any that God brings to your attention.

Do not be surprised if you receive names of people you thought you had already forgiven. Deep wounds leave layers of trauma in their wake, which may require many rounds of forgiveness. Each time you choose to release the offender, another layer is peeled off and you gain access to deeper areas.

Pick one person from the list at a time, and ask the Holy Spirit to show you the effects of their actions upon you. Be honest with yourself about what you have lost as a result of what they did (or didn't do).

1. What emotions and feelings have I experienced as a result?

2. What effects (if any) did this hurt/trauma have on my body?

REMOVING SPIRITUAL BLOCKAGES

> 3. What lies have I been believing as a result of this hurt?
>
> 4. What response(s) have I made, including making inner vows?
>   Which of these might be distortions of God's will for my life?

Pray as follows:

1. _____ (name), I give you the gift of my forgiveness. You owe me nothing. I choose to forgive you for _____ (what they did).

2. _____ (name), I choose to forgive you for the effects of your hurt(s) upon me.

3. I renounce the lies I believed and the inner vows I made. I repent of all ungodly responses I have made to the way you hurt me.

4. Thank you, Father, for setting me free from all the effects of this hurt in every part of my being.

5. I ask you now to bless _____ (name) with _____ (what they need—peace, health, finances, job, business, salvation of loved ones, harmonious relationships, etc.)

You can also use a Scriptural blessing for your offender, such as this passage from Numbers 6:24–26 NKJV:

> "_____ (name), *The Lord bless you and keep you. The Lord make His face shine upon you and be gracious unto you. The Lord lift up His countenance upon you and give you peace.*"

Repeat these steps for everyone the Holy Spirit highlights.

Don't be surprised if more names come to you over the next few days, weeks or months. You have started a process of forgiveness. The Holy Spirit will keep on bringing names to mind. Go through the steps above and set yourself free from any and all unforgiveness you may have been harbouring. Jesus will be pleased with how you have chosen to "forgive from your heart," and you will find yourself walking in new levels of peace and joy.

> You can download a template of the process of "Forgiving from the heart" at www.thesams.ca/resources or by scanning the QR code below:

REMOVING SPIRITUAL BLOCKAGES

REPENTING OF JUDGMENTS

"Do not judge, and you will not be judged. Do not condemn, and you will not be condemned. Forgive, and you will be forgiven" (Luke 6:37).

"He thinks only of himself. When is he ever going to change?"
"She is so controlling!"
"My Dad is such an insensitive boor."
"My Mom is the most vindictive person I know."

Have you ever said such things about someone? These statements we make about others often have an element of truth in them, but they are also judgments we make about another person. It may be true that your father has said insensitive things to you or others before, but by calling him a boor, you are standing in the place of judgement and declaring a verdict. A boomerang effect kicks in when we judge others. Whether we intend it or not, we end up inviting judgment into our lives through the principle of sowing and reaping.

> *A boomerang effect kicks in when we judge others...we end up inviting judgment into our lives.*

> *"Do not be deceived: God cannot be mocked. A man reaps what he sows. Whoever sows to please their flesh, from the flesh will reap destruction; whoever sows to please the Spirit, from the Spirit will reap eternal life. Let us not become weary in doing good, for at the proper time we will reap a harvest if we do not give up. Therefore, as we have opportunity, let us do good to all people, especially to those who belong to the family of believers"* (Galatians 6:7–10).

In the natural realm, when we sow one seed, we reap a harvest that produces way more than we sowed. Just think of what comes up when a farmer plants a grain of wheat or a seed of corn. That is exactly how it is in the spirit realm as well. In this passage in Galatians, Paul is admonishing the community of Jesus-followers to keep doing good, and to treat one another well.

> You sow judgment. You reap more judgment.
>> That is the bad news.
>
> You sow forgiveness. You reap more forgiveness.
>> That is amazing news!

On the surface, judgments feel like a natural way to express the pain from a wound we have experienced. Naming our trauma is certainly valid, you should never keep your pain to yourself just because the way you express your pain may be judgmental in tone. As a matter of fact, naming the hurt is essential to healing (as you will see in Chapter 6—Restoring Peace Following Conflict). The trouble starts when we move from naming our injustice into labeling the offender. When we are tempted to make judgments, we need to remember that we are not called to judge. God makes it very clear that He alone is the judge, and we are to leave all judgments in His hands. He is a God of justice. *"There is only one Lawgiver and Judge, the One who is able to save and to destroy; but who are you who judge your neighbour?"* (James 4:12)

In the book *Grace & Forgiveness*, Carol Arnott shares a dramatic illustration of what can happen when we repent of judgments. She had grown up with an abusive mother who refused to take responsibility for her actions. Carol had already forgiven her repeatedly for the abuse of the past, as well as her ongoing cruelty in the present. She continued to pray for her mother, but it seemed as though their relationship was deteriorating even more.

Eventually, the Holy Spirit convicted Carol of the ways in which she continued to judge her mother, even though she had forgiven her. Once Carol took this conviction to heart and repented of the judgments she had made against her mother, an inexplicable shift took place. Carol's mother voluntarily asked her to forgive her for the way she had treated her! Their relationship was restored in a supernatural way. We make this little book required reading for couples in our marriage mentorship. Some of these couples have shared similar testimonies of relationships being restored as well.

A woman we know who had been estranged from her father for over 10 years took this teaching seriously. She repented for the judgments she had made against her father for leaving her mother and cutting himself off from any contact with their family. A few days later, her father called her "out-of-the-blue," for no reason at all and they had a lovely conversation. God restored their relationship!

In another instance, a man's father had not talked to him personally for decades. He would not even send him a birthday card. Three days after he repented of the judgments he had made, his father shocked him with a phone call to wish him Happy Father's Day! The man told us that his father had never ever offered him Father's Day greetings before. Wow! Once again, we were awestruck by how repenting of judgments led to breakthrough.

While we cannot guarantee that everyone who has been judging others will experience such dramatic results, we pray that these testimonies will spur you to take action by repenting and handing your pain over to God, knowing that He is the righteous judge.

Action Steps

> Take some time now and ask God to show you anyone you have judged in the past, as well as who you may still be judging today. Write down every name that He brings to mind.
>
> Then pray: "Father, I do not want to reap judgment and condemnation against me by the judgments I have sowed against anyone. You alone are the righteous judge. I give

> up my right to judge others. I repent of the sin of judging _____ (list all names the Holy Spirit brought to mind). I repent of judging them with my words, in my thoughts and in my heart. I ask you to forgive me and set me free from the consequences of my sin. I also ask you to cause those harvests of judgment to wither, dry up and die, so that they can produce no more fruit."
>
> Take a moment to receive the forgiveness God offers, and then continue:
>
> "I thank you, Father, for forgiving me and removing all judgments and condemnation that I had invited into my life. I praise you that none of these judgments will ever again boomerang in my face and prevent me from experiencing my breakthrough. In Jesus' mighty name. Amen."

FORGIVING YOURSELF

Some people find that even after turning to God, repenting, and asking for forgiveness, and moving towards forgiveness with others, they are still not at peace. Deep down in their heart, they are not convinced that they have been forgiven. This could very well be because they have not forgiven themselves.

Here is an illustration:

> A husband is experiencing serious complications from diabetes. He realizes that he contributed to the onset of diabetes by his overindulgence of sweets and soft drinks. He has asked God to forgive him for abusing his body, but he has great difficulty forgiving himself for doing all that he did. He is constantly haunted by thoughts such as, "Why did I do that to myself? Look at all the pain I'm causing my wife and children now as a result!"

This is a classic example of someone who has not forgiven himself. Here is another example:

> A woman commits adultery against her husband. She has since repented of her sin. She is totally sure that she has received God's forgiveness. Yet, she keeps on wondering, "Why did I not resist the temptation? Why did I not cut off the relationship before it went too far? Look at how I destroyed the trust in our marriage!" She continues to be plagued by guilt, even though she has been forgiven by God.

Forgiving ourselves can be difficult. We each have an arsenal of memories of our own failures and shortcomings. You may have neglected to visit an elderly parent who dies unexpectedly. Or you were at fault in an accident that severely impacted the life of an innocent victim. The enemy loves to point these out to us and make us feel unworthy of forgiveness and love.

REMOVING SPIRITUAL BLOCKAGES

Sometimes we go on to make judgments about ourselves as well:

"I give in to temptation too quickly."
"I can never get over what I did."
"I cannot forgive myself."
"How could I be so stupid?"

As with forgiving others, forgiving yourself does not absolve you of the responsibility for the problems you caused. Your actions may still have repercussions. But sitting in a place of judgment and self-hatred will not help you move towards healing and wholeness. Even as you repented of judgments you made against others, you now need to repent of any judgments you may have made about yourself as well, and learn to accept God's words over you as your real identity.

Action Steps

1. As you read these words, you may already be aware of some things for which you have not fully forgiven yourself. Write them down.

2. Go ahead and pray: "Holy Spirit, what else do I need to forgive myself for?" Write down whatever you receive in response.

3. Pray: "What judgments (if any) have I made about myself as a result?"

Then offer this prayer:

> "Lord, I choose today to give myself a gift of my own forgiveness. _____ (your own name), I forgive you for _____ (read your list). I let it all go. I will not beat myself up about it anymore. I release it to you, Lord Jesus. I cannot be the Saviour for myself. Lord, you are my Saviour. I repent for making judgments about myself such as _____ (list all that the Holy Spirit showed you). I ask you to forgive me and set me free from the consequences of my judgments."
>
> Take a moment to receive His forgiveness. If these judgmental thoughts return, remind yourself that no matter what happened, you cannot undo the past. You have also chosen to repent, and decided to leave the matter with Jesus.

FORGIVING GOD

Have you ever blamed God for your situation? Did you ever feel that He let you down or chose not to do something about your condition, when perhaps He could have? We do not believe God has ever actually done wrong, but when we sit in judgment on God, it can certainly seem that He has done wrong *by us*. This is often true in the cases of deep tragedy, such as the untimely death of a loved one, the onset of cancer or some other deadly disease, a natural disaster, a wrongful dismissal, a judgment against you despite your innocence, or any unanswered prayer. We simply do not understand why such things happen and somehow, God often seems silent.

Let us make something perfectly clear first. God is a good father. He does not willingly inflict harm upon His children. Yes, He disciplines His children as any good father would (Proverbs 3:12, Hebrews 12:6), but not with disease, destruction, or disaster as punishment. It simply does not align with God's character or His love for us. There is suffering in this world, but it brings God no joy to see us suffer. The truth of the matter is that when we hurt, God hurts with us, as any good father would when his child is experiencing pain and suffering.

Since it is not easy for us to reconcile the goodness of God with the "undeserved" suffering that we sometimes experience, we may feel that God has wronged us. And when we feel that God has wronged us, we cannot experience total intimacy with Him. It is as though there is a barrier standing between us and Him. For the sake of our healing, therefore, there may be times when we need to "forgive" God for things that happen to us that we do not fully understand. We also may need to give up our right to understand why.

Action Steps

Pray: "Holy Spirit, will you reveal to me all instances where I have blamed you for what happened in my life?" Write them all down.

Then pray:

"Lord, I have blamed You for things that have happened to me and the circumstances of my life, such as

> _____. Today I am choosing to stop demanding an explanation before I can move on. You are a good God and someday I will understand a bigger picture that I cannot comprehend right now. I confess that holding this blame against you is wrong. I repent and ask you to forgive me. I release all my questions to you and today I choose to trust. I thank you for your patience and limitless love and I accept your mercy and grace. In Jesus' name. Amen."

Take a moment to receive His forgiveness and peace.

Whew! You've just completed some powerful processes in the spirit realm and removed several spiritual blockages preventing your breakthrough. Let us keep going till we take care of every possible impediment to intimacy with God that we are aware of.

BREAKING OFF UNGODLY TIES

In life we have many relationships, beginning with the one between us as children and our parents, and other members of the family. As time goes on, we have relationships with friends, then boyfriends/girlfriends, spouses, coworkers, etc. Along the way we also develop relationships with certain people in authority such as teachers, coaches, mentors, pastors and other leaders. When these relationships are healthy and life-giving, we establish bonds of trust and love that enhance our well-being. When these relationships turn sour or downright toxic, then ungodly ties can bind us to one another, causing ongoing trauma.

In relationships where one person exercises undue (ungodly) control over the other, whether spiritually, emotionally or physically, ungodly soul ties can form. For example, a parent who continues to control a married child; a pastor who forbids a member from associating with anyone outside of their church; a teacher who abuses a student; a manipulative mentor who makes you dependent upon them alone for counsel; or a possessive friend who tries to isolate you from other friends and control everything you do.

An ungodly soul tie can also be established when a person willingly gives undue access to their soul to someone. Examples could be a father who gets so enmeshed in the life of a child and neglects his own wife in the process; a wife who is still so attached to her father that she keeps on reaching out to him for help instead of her husband; a young woman preparing for marriage who is still tied in her thoughts to previous lovers; or a man who develops an obsession with a girl pictured on a porn site.

When there is sexual activity outside of the marriage covenant, we believe an ungodly spirit, soul and bodily tie is established. This includes sexual activity as an unmarried person (single, separated, divorced, widowed) and while being married.

The reason we call these "ties" is because they connect you in a strong way to another person and hinder you from fully connecting intimately with your spouse. You have been held back in your thoughts, emotions, will, desire or body in ways that keep you from sharing yourself wholly. It is as though you were trying to run a race while dragging a few other people with you, whether you meant to or not. In order to accelerate toward your breakthrough, you need to break off these unhealthy and ungodly spirit, soul and bodily ties, while holding on to the good, life-giving aspects of those relationships that nurtured you.

Action Steps

Pray: "Holy Spirit, will you show me the people with whom I have established an ungodly, unhealthy spirit, soul or bodily tie all through my life? Whether caused by their sin or my sin, please highlight these people to me." Write down each name.

Then pray: "In the name of Jesus, I break off all unhealthy and ungodly spirit, soul or bodily ties that were established between me and _____ (names), whether in my mind, through my will, emotions or my body. God, I ask you to free me from any evil perpetrated by others. I repent for any way I have contributed to these ties being established myself. I release to the other person any part of them that remains in me that is rightfully theirs, cleansed by the blood of Jesus. I repossess any part of me that remains in them that is rightfully mine, cleansed by the blood of Jesus.

Because you are the God of redemption, I declare that what the enemy meant for harm, you will turn to good as I walk in obedience to you in the days ahead. Thank you for restoring and making me new by your power. Holy

> Spirit, come now and seal this restoration you have done in my spirit, soul and body. In Jesus' name. Amen."
>
> If you still have any objects in your possession that remind you of the person with whom you established this tie (e.g. love letters, journals, cards, gifts, jewelry, charms or clothing), we strongly suggest you get rid of them, so they do not continue to reinforce any unhealthy, ungodly, spirit, soul, bodily tie that may have been established.

BREAKING OFF GENERATIONAL HINDRANCES

Have you ever wondered why the same patterns or behaviours keep on recurring in succeeding generations of a family? For example, a disproportionately high number of children of addicts become addicts themselves. Certain diseases and conditions also follow a generational pattern—e.g. cancer, diabetes, heart disease, anxiety, depression, suicidal tendencies, etc. We often hear people casually say things like, "Diabetes runs in my family." Some of this can be explained by genetics. In other words, it is passed down generational lines in the DNA. The science of epigenetics explains how our environment and our choices can influence our genetic code

The tendency to commit the same sin can be transmitted down through generational lines.

and that of succeeding generations, changing how our bodies read our DNA. Beyond genetics and epigenetics, however, we are also alerted to generational hindrances in Scripture.

The earliest reference is found among the Ten Commandments where God says He will *"visit the iniquity of the fathers upon the children unto the third and fourth generation of them that hate me"* (Exodus 20:5 KJV). It is important to understand that this is not a punishment. After all, elsewhere in Scripture God makes it clear that He will not punish a person for their parents' sins (see Deuteronomy 24:6 and Ezekiel 18:4). One interpretation of the word iniquity is "the tendency to sin." In other words, the tendency to commit the same sin can be transmitted down through generational lines.

These repeating patterns are what we call generational hindrances. In other words, someone in a previous generation opened the door for the enemy to get in. And those tendencies continue to be passed down through the generations, until someone stands in the gap, repents and asks God to remove them (as we see in Nehemiah 9:1–2 and Daniel 9:1–19).

As you read this, you might already be able to identify generational hindrances which have manifested in your family line, affecting your life or the lives of your siblings and other members of your family. The scary part is that if these are not removed, they could continue to affect your children, their children and succeeding generations. The good part is that through your relationship to God and the power of the Cross, you have been given authority to break them off once and for all.

It is also entirely possible that you cannot come up with a list. Or you may not be able to go back more than a generation or two. Do not fret too much if you are unable to find this information, just work with what you are able to glean from your family, what you see manifesting in your life right now, and what you sense might be generational in origin. The main thing is to remove all such hindrances to your breakthrough.

Action Steps

What generational hindrances are you aware of in your family line? Write them all down. Consider both your father's and your mother's generational lines. Go as far back as you possibly can. You may need help from your parents, grandparents or other family members to compile this list.

Here is a prayer that you can use to break off all ungodly generational hindrances.

"In the name of Jesus, and by the power of His blood, I now break off all generational hindrances I have inherited from all my ancestors known to me, such as _____ (list them all) and others that are unknown to me. I place the cross of Christ between me and the sins of my ancestors. In the name of Jesus, I command all demonic oppression that has come down my ancestral lines to end right now. And I take back every generational blessing that has been withheld from me. Holy Spirit, come now and set your seal of freedom upon me and my future generations. In Jesus' name. Amen."

PARENTAL BLESSINGS

Earlier, when you asked the Holy Spirit to show you who you needed to forgive, chances are very high that your parents were on that list. You may have also repented for sowing dishonour by the judgments you made about them. This is extremely significant, as it carries consequences:

> *"Honour your father and your mother, as the LORD your God has commanded you, so that you may live long and it may go well with you in the land that the LORD your God is giving you"* (Deuteronomy 5:16).

When you forgave them from the heart, we hope you also asked God to bless them with what they need. These acts of forgiveness and repentance have removed some serious blockages to your breakthrough already. But there is one more thing connected to parents that can be a powerful factor in your life—it has to do with the power of your parents' blessing.

The Scriptural basis for parental blessing is found in the book of Genesis. We see repeatedly that one of the most significant acts a father can do is to bless his sons. Abraham blessed Isaac who blessed Jacob who, in turn, blessed his sons. There is a poignant scene in Genesis 27, where Esau realizes that his younger brother Jacob had deceived their father Isaac into giving him the blessing that rightfully belonged to the oldest son. He cries out: *"Do you have only one blessing, my father? Bless me too, my father!"* Then Esau wept aloud (Genesis 27:38). Very clearly, Esau understood the power of his father's blessing upon his destiny.

What constitutes a parental blessing? These are simply words of life, affirmation and destiny meant to be delivered to you from God's heart through your parents. God knew you and planned a special purpose for you before you were even in your mother's womb. He wanted you to know, from a very early age, the great pleasure that you brought to His heart before you were even able to do anything for Him. Words of blessing impart life and hope and change the way we think about ourselves. They convey the perspective of heaven about who we are (our identity), and where we are meant to go (our destiny) in life.

Look at what God does right after creating human beings, male and female, in His image.

> *"Then God blessed them, and God said to them, 'Be fruitful and multiply; fill the earth and subdue it; have dominion over the fish of the sea, over the birds of the air, and over every living thing that moves on the earth'"* (Genesis 1:28 **NKJV**).

The ability to 'have dominion' comes after you are blessed.

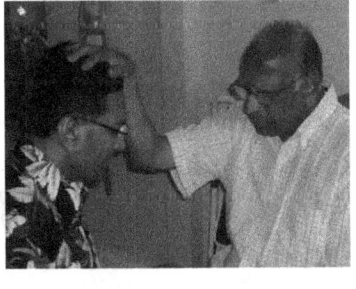

A number of years ago, I (Jeeva) realized that I had been living without my father's blessing all my adult life. At our Thanksgiving gathering that year, I asked my Dad to lay hands on me and bless me. It was one of the most spiritually significant moments of my life. That simple act of blessing has released multiple gifts into our lives—an increase in anointing, business ventures and ministry opportunities, to name a few.

My (Sulojana's) father passed away in 1984, so I never received a personal blessing from him as Jeeva did. Several years ago, at a pastors' gathering, our spiritual father, Pastor Steve Long, released a father's blessing to me. I have experienced a greater freedom and boldness to minister in public since that time and to launch new initiatives such as a prayer group in my workplace.

We do not know exactly how or why parental blessing works, we simply know it does. We understand that some of you were hurt by the way your parents raised you and treated you. Whether they were responding out of the unhealed hurts they carried at the time or were simply cruel for no discernible reason, you may find it difficult to come to terms with our assertion that you need their blessing. Truth be told, they need to ask for your forgiveness and they should own their actions, though sadly, this does not always happen.

While you may not be able to honour your parents as god-fearing people who were a source of blessing, you can still acknowledge them simply for being your parents, and blessing you with the gift of life. You can still ask them to release a blessing if they are willing to do so. We also understand that some parents are not able or equipped to release their blessing at the appropriate time but can deliver later, as with Jeeva. Otherwise, a godly friend, mentor or pastor can do this for you, as with Sulojana. Some whose parents are still alive will not offer that blessing because they are not believers, or they are believers who do not fully understand the power of the blessing. Don't let this hold you back, the blessing comes from God after all, and He can release it to you through someone else.

We have noticed that of the many couples who have come through our Marriage Mentorship Process, virtually none of them had ever received a blessing from their parents. As a matter of fact, quite often what they received was the opposite. We have often stood in the place of their father and mother and released parental blessings. Every time we have done this, it has been a powerful, moving experience for everyone involved.

Action Steps

> Since this could be a key element that contributes to breakthrough in your marriage, we urge you to find a way to receive a parental blessing. The best option is for your birth father and mother or adopted parents to bless you. Feel free to use the blessings (pdf) from www.thesams.ca/resources or scan the QR code below.
>
> The next best option is for your spiritual father/mother or pastor or mentor to release it to you.
>
> If neither of the above is an option for you, feel free to use the audio recordings available at the website listed above.

No matter how you do it, please ensure that you receive your parental blessings on the way to receiving your breakthrough.

There is one more key element that you need to be aware of in the spirit realm before we get to addressing matters of the soul. It is about being in alignment with God's design for us.

ALIGNMENT

What do you think of when you hear the word "alignment?"

I (Jeeva) remember taking my car for an oil change many years ago. As the car was up on the hoist, the mechanic was doing a visual inspection. He pointed out to me that the two front tires needed to be replaced because they had worn out unevenly. Sure enough, even I, a mechanically challenged man, could see the uneven wear of the tread. Then he explained the underlying cause: the wheels were out of alignment! He asked me if I'd noticed the car veering off to one side when I was driving on the highway and if I had to keep on bringing it back on to the pavement. I certainly had. He advised me to get a wheel alignment right after I replaced the tires. Had I made a $100 investment in an alignment earlier, I could have saved nearly $300 in tire replacement charges.

REMOVING SPIRITUAL BLOCKAGES

Similarly, there is an alignment that God has designed for marriage that we are wise to observe. When you are out of alignment with God's design, you too could be wearing each other out. Your marriage is not staying straight on the highway of life and could veer off the road altogether. At that point, it becomes a very expensive fix. Getting in alignment now is preferable to paying the price later!

> **When you are out of alignment with God's design, you too could be wearing each other out.**

What is this alignment? Here is how the apostle Paul states it: *"The head of every man is Christ, the head of woman is man, and the head of Christ is God"* (1 Corinthians 11:3, NKJV).

This graphic illustrates the alignment:

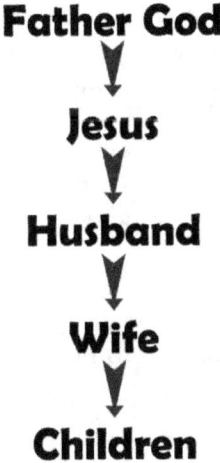

What is the key to making this alignment work? When we read through Ephesians 5:21–33, we realize that it is submission.

> Jesus was in alignment with His Father by being in submission to God as His head.
> The Church is in alignment with Jesus by submitting to Him as its head.
> The husband is in alignment with Jesus by submitting to Him as his head.
> The wife is in alignment with her husband by submitting to him as her head.
> The children are in alignment by submitting to their parents as their head.

Defining Headship

Before we go any further, we need to get an accurate picture of what Paul means by "head" in this passage. He is not talking about the head of a corporation, hierarchy, or monarchy. He is talking about a head that is connected to a body, that is part of the body itself and is responsible for caring for it. Jesus is the head of His body, the Church. The husband is the head of his body, his wife. There is no superiority or domination implied by this image. The head has a function that is impossible to fulfil without the body and the body needs the head to function at all.

Please pay attention also as to how the husband is supposed to exercise his headship. He is to love his wife as Christ loved the Church, i.e. by laying down his life for her. That is the farthest you can get from domination, control, and demanding submission. Husbands, when you treat your wife with sacrificial love, she will see Jesus in you, and will find it easy to submit to you as the head.

Defining Submission

I (Sulojana) am often asked how I could be in submission to my husband. This often stems from a fearful expectation of what submission means. Submitting does not make me a doormat! I want to honour God's design for marriage, and I believe the right thing for me to do is to acknowledge Jeeva as the head of our marriage and submit to him. After all, anything with two heads is a monster! As my head, my husband serves me and cares for me. He does not walk all over me or rule me with an iron fist. Jesus would never do that and neither will Jeeva. Let us illustrate how this works from two incidents in our lives where we had to make key decisions.

A few years ago, Jeeva wanted to hire a coach to help us launch our Marriage Mentorship Process. Because he loves me as Christ loved the Church, he did not go ahead and hire that person on his own. He consulted me and asked for my input. I did not feel totally comfortable with the investment required, so I let him know that. Jeeva took that into consideration and did not hire the coach.

A few weeks later, he brought it up again. I was still not fully convinced that we needed to invest in a coach, but since Jeeva felt that it would be really helpful, I left the decision to him. In other words, I let him know that I was submitting to his headship in this matter. And no matter what he decided,

I would be OK with it. This time, he went ahead and hired the coach. It turned out to be a great decision for launching our Marriage Mentorship Process.

We also put into practice what Paul says in the passage cited earlier, *"Submit yourself to one another out of reverence to Christ"* (Ephesians 5:21). In 2005, we received word that our landlord had decided to put up for sale the house we were renting and we would need to find new accommodations. I (Jeeva) wanted to keep on renting, but Sulojana was sure that this was God's way of telling us to buy our own home. I was reluctant at first, but eventually submitted to her. We ended up buying the house in which we live right now. Over the past 15 years, it has tripled in value. In this case, it literally paid to submit to one another!

The Place Of Children

We have included children on our diagram of alignment, below the wife, honouring the order we see in this passage of scripture:

> *"Your wife will be like a fruitful vine within your house; Your children will be like olive shoots around your table. Yes, this will be the blessing for the man who fears the Lord"* (Psalm 128:3–4).

We have often seen couples put their children ahead of their spouse in priority. In catering to the needs of their children, they ignore the needs of their spouse and put themselves out of alignment. It is true that at certain stages of life children will demand a large amount of our time and energy, but that still does not make them a higher priority than our spouse. You need to make sure that your spouse knows that they are the most important person in your life. There will come a day when your children will no longer live under your roof, while you and your spouse will still be together. Giving your spouse a higher priority than your children right from the early years will make this later time of your life more enjoyable, as we are discovering now.

Action Steps

> Our pastors Matt & Lisa Tapley preached a message called "Bold Love." You can access it at www.thesams.ca/resources (or scan the QR code below). We suggest you listen to this recording of their message, and then answer these questions:
>
> 1. What points stood out as you listened to the recording? What did the Holy Spirit highlight for you?
>
> 2. The Tapleys mention many expectations God has of husbands and wives. Compare what you heard on the recording with what you saw in your parents' marriage:
>
>   How did they model this for you positively?
>
>   Where did they miss the mark?
>
> 3. Now examine how those expectations are reflected in your own marriage:
>
>   Where are you right on target with God's expectations?

> Where are you missing the mark?
>
> List some practical steps you could each take to ensure that your marriage is in alignment with God's design.
>
> Share your responses with each other.

GOING DEEPER

As you diligently do what we've recommended thus far, you will remove many spiritual blockages on your own without any help from anyone else. You should know though that every couple we have mentored has required personalized inner healing ministry before experiencing the fullest measure of freedom. This could be because many of them were on the brink of divorce by the time they had reached out to us for help. The wounds they carried ran deep—as a result of repeated hurts, trauma or prolonged abuse—often as far back as childhood and sometimes even as a baby in the womb.

Even if you are not at that point, you will likely still find it beneficial to seek outside help. Over 10 years ago, we both invested a week of our lives receiving such healing ministry ourselves using the Restoring The Foundations (RTF) model. This brought much freedom to us individually and greater intimacy between us as a couple. It made us realize that there are no such things as marriage problems, but two individuals with their own personal problems coupled together in a marriage. We also realized that there was another biblical principle which was responsible for the effectiveness of this process.

> *There is a greater measure of healing that comes from confessing our sins in safe community.*

"Therefore, confess your sins to each other and pray for each other so that you may be healed" (James 5:16).

There is a greater measure of healing that comes from confessing our sins in safe community. We believe that the effectiveness of inner healing ministries and professional counselling has much to do with this principle: God has designed us to heal together.

Many people also carry ungodly beliefs and spirit-soul hurts that could be preventing them from experiencing freedom in its fullest possible measure. It is beyond the scope of this book to cover every topic in greater detail. We recommend every couple seriously consider in-person prayer ministry and/or counselling to take care of the deeper issues we all carry.

We also need to alert you that some of you will need further professional help even after receiving such inner healing ministry. If you have experienced lasting trauma, we would highly recommend that you seek out a qualified Christian psychologist or therapist. It is well worth the time and the money you invest in identifying and addressing any residual effects in your being, so that your healing may fully encompass your spirit, soul and body.

Action Steps

> Seek out a reputable team of inner healing ministers from any of the ministries we have mentioned at the back of this book, or others recommended by your pastor. If you'd like us to help you find a team, please reach out to us directly (again, see details at the back of the book).
>
> Seek out a qualified professional Christian therapist. Many therapists can be found at psychology.com and psychologytoday.com.

Congratulations for sticking with the Marriage Mentorship Process so far. You have shifted the spiritual atmosphere in your home. You have removed spiritual blockages in your being. You will begin to realize the impact of what you have done so far in Chapters 3 & 4 in all aspects of your marriage, beginning with Communication.

CHAPTER 5

GROWING IN COMMUNICATION

You have probably heard that good communication is the key to a successful marriage. That is very true. In this short passage from his book *Keep Your Love On*, author Danny Silk sums up why communication is so vital in any healthy relationship, especially marriage:

> "In a respectful relationship, each person understands, 'I am responsible to know what is going on inside me and communicate it to you. I do not expect you to know it, nor will I allow you to assume that you know it. And I will not make assumptions about what is going on inside you.'"

Let us now show you practical ways in which you can communicate with each other.

LEVELS OF COMMUNICATION

First, we need to realize that communication takes place at many different levels in a marriage, each of which bear examining.

At the most basic level, communication is about transmitting information from one person to another.

> "Sweetheart, the doctor's office called to remind you of your appointment tomorrow at 10:30 am."

The next level of communication is sharing your feelings with each other. You are not just transmitting information but also conveying how you feel about it. This is especially important when you are resolving conflict (as we will examine in the next section).

> "I am worried about the results of the ultrasound."

What should set apart communication in a marriage from any other relationship is the freedom to share anything at all with your spouse without fear of being judged, criticized, condemned, or punished for being honest and open about it. If the communication in your marriage does not fit this description right now, no worries. You can learn how to grow in communication, beginning with this simple technique.

Active Listening

> "Everyone should be quick to listen, slow to speak and slow to become angry" (James 5:19).

GROWING IN COMMUNICATION

Listening is more than just hearing what the other person is saying. Active listening is when you repeat in your own words what you just heard your spouse say and ask questions for clarification. Sometimes it is called mirroring as well. It may sound like parroting, but it promotes greater understanding. Let us illustrate:

> Husband: "Honey, I'm going to be working late tonight. My manager wants me to be in the office for a meeting with a client."
> Wife: "You're going to be working late tonight because of a client meeting?"
> Husband: "Yeah, this could be a huge meeting. If we get this contract, we'll have enough orders to keep us going for three years."
> Wife: "Wow! Enough orders to keep you going for three years? That could be quite the contract!!"
> Husband: "Yes, but first we have to close the deal, and I'm not totally sure that we can."
> Wife: "You're not totally sure that you can close the deal. How come?"
> Husband: "We've never closed a deal this big before in our company and my manager is expecting me to get the job done."
> Wife: "Your manager is expecting you to close the deal? Honey, it sounds to me like you're under stress."
> Husband: "Yeah, I'm stressed out about it, to be honest."
> Wife: "Yes, it is stressful for you, but I am totally confident that you'll do the best job possible."
> Husband: "I can definitely do my best. I appreciate your confidence in me, honey."
> Wife: "You're the best! I'll be praying for you. Go, get them!"

By employing active listening and repeating back to your spouse what you understood them to say, you communicate not only that you understood the facts but that you care about them. Active listening can help share the stress load and provide support simply by keeping the conversation going.

Action Steps

Go through these lists of questions that are designed to help you grow in your communication. Allow a few days or a week in between each set of questions. One person begins by reading a question and then listens intently without interrupting while the other person answers. Practise active listening by first repeating what they just told you. Next ask them to clarify anything that is not clear to you. Do not challenge or critique their responses.

Starter Questions

- If you won an all-expenses-paid trip to anywhere in the world, where would you go? Why?
- What are your favourite worship songs, hymns or choruses? Why are they your favourites?
- If you could meet anyone in the Bible, who would it be? Why? What would you ask them?
- What is one question you want God to answer? Why this one?
- Who are your heroes or people you have looked up to over the years? What makes them special to you?
- Describe two of your favourite memories of things we have done together.

Next Level Questions

- How are you like your Dad? Your Mom?
- How are you different from your Dad? Your Mom?
- What other relatives were important to you growing up? Why?
- What is something you have never done that you would like to try? Why?
- What is something that scares you that you would never ever try? Why?
- What all is on your "bucket list"?
- Imagine your life 10 years from now. What excites you about growing older? What scares you about it?

Deeper Questions

- What are you really excited about right now? (Personally, in the family, work/business, church, country, etc.)
- What are you really scared about right now in the same areas?
- Share something new you have learned recently (about God, yourself, your spouse, family, work/business, the world)
- Share any dreams you have had during the night recently that you would consider significant. Do you have any idea what they might mean?
- Who in our family and friendship circles are you concerned about? How shall we pray for them?
- If you have received personal prophecies, listen again to any recordings you may have, or read any

written records/transcriptions.[13] Which prophecies can you see becoming reality? Do any of them sound too good to be true? What changes do you need to make to partner with the Holy Spirit to fulfill these prophecies?

TRANSPARENCY

If there is a distinguishing mark of communication that a couple must aim to achieve in their marriage, it might well be transparency. We like to say that transparency is the key that unlocks the door to intimacy. Keeping secrets about past relationships, financial matters, traumatic events, abuses, and so on, erodes trust. Being transparent with each other means holding no secrets from each other. Secrets create barriers. Removing those barriers promotes transparency.

> *Transparency is the key that unlocks the door to intimacy.*

Transparency is about exposing the good, the bad and the ugly. Even when some of what is revealed may be painful for the other spouse to accept, it is better for you to risk being open with each other rather than carrying the burden of these

---

[13] Personal prophecies are words of encouragement or guidance from God given through a person who hears them and shares them with you. This is commonplace in many Pentecostal and Charismatic churches. If you have never received a word of personal prophecy and would like to, see our list of resources at the end of the book.

secrets by yourself. Give each other grace as you go through this process of developing total transparency.

When you are totally transparent with each other about your past, you never have to worry about any secrets from your past haunting you in the future. There will be no surprises that can rattle your marriage. As Jesus said: *"For all that is secret will eventually be brought into the open, and everything that is concealed will be brought to light and made known to all"* (Luke 8:17 NLT). Is it not better for the two of you to bring secrets to light rather than have someone else bring them out into the open?

When you share your past with each other, you gain greater appreciation for what your spouse went through before your paths crossed. This will help you treat them with greater compassion and provide the support they need in their journey of healing from those hurts. That being said, we would caution you that there are times when open transparency could cause such deep hurt that it could have a negative impact on your marriage. For example, we have witnessed how disclosing sexual relationships outside of marriage devastated the other spouse so much that it threatened a breakup. We would advise you to reveal such potentially damaging secrets in the presence of a caring third party such as your pastor or other qualified professional, if possible. You also need to be prepared for a prolonged period of healing.

Even with all these potentially painful consequences, you will still discover that transparency enhances intimacy.

Action Steps

Here is an exercise called "The Life Line", which will help you practise transparency.

1. Take a sheet of paper and orient it in "landscape" format, with the long side on the top and bottom. Draw a horizontal line in the middle of the paper from one end to the other. (Use the template in the workbook: www.thesams.ca/resources)

2. On the far left edge, enter "0" to mark your birth. At the far right edge, enter your current age.

3. Ask the Holy Spirit to highlight key events that have shaped your life—both highs and lows. Mark high points above the line and low points below the line. High points might include significant events, achievements, graduation, marriage, jobs, the birth of a child, etc. Low points might include disappointments, failures, moves, breakup, divorce, hurts or losses. Do not hold anything back.

4. Write a couple of words to describe each point and mark your age/year at each of the high & low points.

5. Draw lines connecting the points (see illustration below)

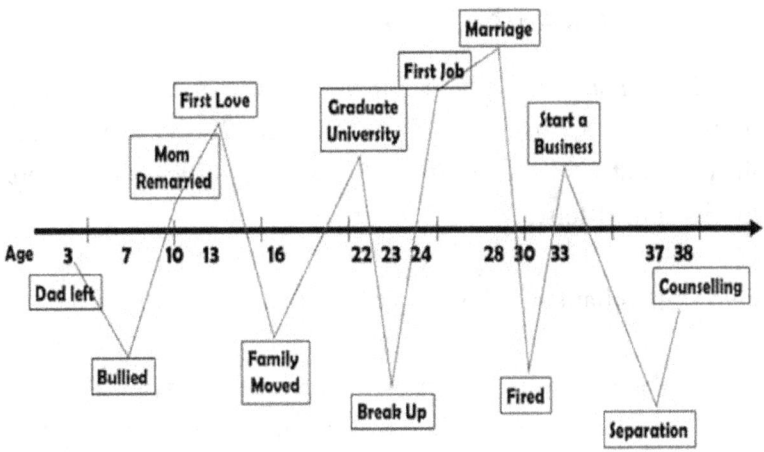

Share with each other the details of every item on both the upper and lower portions. As your spouse shares, respond with active listening. Ask questions for clarification. Be careful not to judge them. Remember, the goal is total transparency with empathy and compassionate, non-judgmental listening.

Celebrate the positives and celebrate God's grace and favour that were evident in those events. Share any unresolved hurts that remain from any of these memories/events. Help each other receive healing using the tools in the previous section for removing spiritual blockages as necessary. Seek out professional help should you need deeper healing.

You will be amazed by how transparency increases intimacy in your marriage!

PHRASING YOUR HURT WELL

Finally, transparency also requires you to communicate your hurts to your spouse. How do you do this? There are two key phrases that need to be part of this communication: "When you..." and "I felt..."

Two things happen when you phrase your hurt this way:

1. Your spouse now knows exactly what **they did** that hurt you. You are being transparent. You are pointing it out to them, but you are doing so in a way that does not accuse or condemn.
2. You are letting them know how **you felt** as a result of their hurt. When someone tells us how they are feeling, we should never tell them that they should not feel that way. The best response is to acknowledge their feeling before we do anything else.

Let us apply this phrasing to some situations that couples often run into.

> "*When you* came home late without letting me know why you were delayed, *I felt* worried, upset, angry."

> "*When you* bought that new TV without both of us discussing it together, *I felt* left out, unimportant, _____ (fill in the blanks.)"

> "*When you* booked that weekend off with your girlfriends without checking with me first, *I felt* insignificant, undervalued, angry, etc."

GROWING IN COMMUNICATION

If you have trouble finding the right "feeling" words, consult the Feelings Chart in this section.

There may be times when you do not feel confident or comfortable enough to share your hurt with your spouse face to face. In such instances, you can also write a note using the same phrasing as above and leave it in a place where they are sure to notice it and read it.

Keep on practising what we have shared in this segment, and you will keep on growing in communication with each other.

> For additional discussion questions on this chapter and to download a pdf of the Feelings Chart, go to www.thesams.ca/resources or scan the QR code below:

FEELINGS CHART

GROWING IN COMMUNICATION

FURTHER COMMUNICATION ACTIVITIES

Wedding Day Memories

Find your wedding album or photos from your wedding day. Go through them together. If you have a video/movie, you can watch it as well. Enjoy reliving the memories of that day. Complete these sentences as you share from your heart with each other.

1. When I gazed into your eyes that day, I felt…
2. Some of the thoughts that went through my mind were…
3. The most memorable thing for me about our wedding was…
4. The funniest memory I have about our wedding day is…
5. What I miss in our marriage today that we had on our wedding day is/are…

Pick out at least one picture from your wedding album that shows both of you looking happy. If you can, also pick out at least two more pictures that show you both really enjoying life together—on vacation, with children, a special birthday, anniversary, etc.

Put these up on the fridge or in some other prominent location where you will see them several times a day. You could make one of these photos the background on the screen of your computer/tablet/phone so you will see it every time you open up that device (if you're unsure how to do this, find a young person to help you!).

This activity not only helps you communicate at a deeper level, it also imprints in your brain images of how God intends you to enjoy each other in your marriage. Repeated exposure to these images aids in the process of translating those pictures from the past into present day reality.

Sharing Your Gratitude Journal

Take the gratitude journal that you have been keeping since you began the Marriage Mentorship Process. Share with each other every answer you have written to the question: "What is one thing about my spouse that I am thankful for today?" Look each other in the eye as much as possible during this sharing. One spouse begins by reading all the reasons from their journal. Then the other spouse shares all their entries. Overwhelm each other with gratitude.

You can weave them into a prayer at the end, if you would like, such as, "Lord, I thank you for _____. I thank you that he/she _____."

CHAPTER 6

RESTORING PEACE FOLLOWING CONFLICT

CONFLICT IS INEVITABLE

Every marriage has its share of conflict. By itself, conflict is not bad. It is actually a sign that you are communicating openly with each other. However, times of conflict can turn ugly when we allow our emotions to dictate our actions. Quite often, when you are in the middle of a heated argument, you are likely to say and do things that you might regret later. After this, it becomes more difficult to work through the hurt.

In times like these, when you begin to feel your blood boiling, your temperature rising, your palms sweating, your body shaking, or whatever other symptom that signals to you that you are headed for a blow out, here is what you can do.

Call A Timeout

This is very similar to a timeout that gets called in the middle of a game. Sometimes coaches call one when they can sense that letting their team continue playing would be detrimental to the outcome—either because of physical or mental fatigue, or if they are not sticking to their game plan. Sometimes players take the initiative. For example, the quarterback in a football game calls a timeout because he sees a different defensive formation and is not sure how to handle it. Either way, a timeout is a temporary interval that can change the permanent outcome of a game, if it is handled properly. The same is true of conflict between a husband and a wife.

Just as in sports, all it takes is for one person to call the timeout. Whoever feels that the situation could be getting out of hand first calls the timeout. The other person may not be ready for the timeout. You may want to keep on going, but if your spouse calls one, you need to oblige.

The second important thing to notice about a timeout is that there is a definite duration to it. That is the "time" part of the "timeout." In sports, timeouts are usually a minute or less. You may need an hour or more to cool down. Longer periods are fine—a few hours or even a day is OK. The main thing is that there is a definite duration that you agree on, and you get back together at the agreed time to discuss the matter.

Sometimes your conflict may result in a cold war rather than a heated battle. You know that you need to make your spouse aware of how they hurt you, but you don't do it. You are afraid that sharing your feelings openly will cause further friction or hurt, so you let those hurts simmer deep inside without expressing them. This is equally unhealthy. Eventually, they will come out like a volcanic eruption and end up causing far more damage.

We will lead you through a 3-part process that will ultimately result in restoration of peace—whether you had to endure a blow-out or an uneasy calm.

THE PROCESS OF RESTORING PEACE

This process follows the Spirit-Soul-Body connection that we discussed at the outset of this book. Here is the picture, as a reminder:

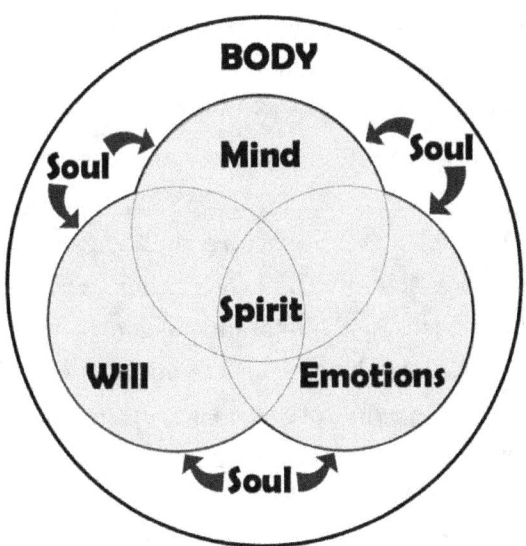

1. Begin in the spirit realm, asking and receiving forgiveness from God first. Then privately release forgiveness to your spouse.
2. Next move to the soul realm where you face your spouse in person, admit the hurt you caused, acknowledge the feelings aroused by it and ask them to forgive you.

3. Finally, involve both the soul and the body realm in coming up with a written plan to ensure that the issue behind the conflict is dealt with constructively.

In our experience, involving all three realms results in restoring peace in a holistic way. Often, we find couples trying to restore peace in one or two of these realms only. While that can lead to a temporary calm, it typically does not lead to lasting peace. Let us explain why.

Sometimes, a couple will stay in the spirit realm alone, praying about the conflict and asking God to restore peace. That is a good first step, but if prayer alone restored peace, Christians would not need marriage coaches, counselors, mentors, or therapists!

Some other couples try to restore the peace entirely in the soul realm. They acknowledge each other's feelings, do their best not to rehash past hurts and decide to move past the conflict. This will produce results temporarily, but is also not sufficient if you have not forgiven each other or come up with a plan to prevent it from recurring.

Some rush to offer a quick apology, promise never to commit the offense again, and then kiss and make-up. It may look like peace has been restored in the physical realm, but chances are good that it will not have staying power, because the hurts in the soul realm have not been acknowledged and forgiveness has not been extended in the spirit realm.

We will illustrate this for you with an incident from our own life.

The Big Chill

One day, Sulojana and I (Jeeva) were having a conversation over Skype with her family in Malaysia. She was sitting in front of the computer, and I was standing in the background facing the stove, with my back to the laptop. As she was talking, her sister asked, "What is Jeeva doing behind you in the kitchen?"

"He's cooking," Sulojana explained.
"Jeeva's cooking?!" her sister asked, shocked.
"If I don't cook, we don't eat," I answered.

Sulojana's family laughed. I laughed. Sulojana laughed. It was all one big joke. Right? Wrong! The minute the Skype call ended, the temperature in the room suddenly dropped 65 degrees. It turned icy cold!

"Why would you say that to my family?" Sulojana demanded.
"Say what?" I asked, in ignorance.
"That if you don't cook, we don't eat."
"Sulojana, that was a joke!"
"That was NOT a joke."
"But they laughed!" I defended.
"I know they did, but you left them with the impression that I don't do any cooking around here, that you do it all."

Sulojana huffed, before storming out of the room. I stood there not sure what to do. She was clearly hurt by what I said.

What are some possible ways we could deal with this hurt?

I (Sulojana) could have said: "You have no idea how you hurt me, do you? For you everything is a joke. Let me tell you something, it isn't funny to me at all. When are you ever going to learn to stop putting me down in front of others? You just keep on doing this like it has no impact on me. You are so insensitive! Men…"

Would that have led to a positive outcome? Not likely! When you run into a situation such as this in your marriage, how do you go from here to restoring peace? Here's what ended up happening.

Take a timeout

We called a timeout (as suggested earlier) and agreed to meet at the end of the day. Here is what we did during the timeout.

Begin in the spirit realm

We shifted the spiritual atmosphere by simply saying: "Holy Spirit, come!"

Next, we took our thoughts captive. The thought came to me (Sulojana): "How dare he keep on putting you down in front of others?" Rather than come into agreement with that thought, I immediately applied the

H.A.L.T method, Holding that thought, Arresting it, Locking it up with Jesus, and Thanking Jesus for taking it from me.

At the same time, Jeeva also applied H.A.L.T to the thought that came to him, which was: "She made such a big fuss about something so small! You're not going to let her get away with it, are you?"

We then moved to receiving forgiveness from God and releasing forgiveness to each other.

Receiving & releasing forgiveness

I intentionally forgave Jeeva for hurting me, whether he had intended to or not. "I choose to forgive you, Jeeva, for putting me down in front of my family. I give you the gift of my forgiveness. Forgive me, Father, for the way I lashed out at him." I paused for a moment to reflect and receive God's forgiveness.

Jeeva did the same, "I choose to forgive you, Sulojana, for the angry way in which you responded to what I thought was a harmless joke. Forgive me, Lord, for the hurt I caused Sulojana with my witty response."

Next, we repented of judgments we had made against each other, asking God to forgive us and release us from the consequences of our sin. Once we had dealt with the hurt in the spirit realm (in private), we were ready to move on to the soul realm and into reconciliation (in person).

The process of reconciliation

The timeout had ended. We came back together. Jeeva led the conversation:

> "Sulojana, I hurt you by telling your family that if I don't cook, we don't eat. Did I get that right?"
> "Yes," I replied.
> "Sulojana, this is how you must have felt as a result—upset, hurt, angry, mad, frustrated, and put down. Did I identify all your feelings? Did I leave any out?"
> "You got most of them, Jeeva. I also felt belittled."
> "Thank you for adding that. I am sorry you also felt belittled. I feel awful, bad, sad, and disappointed in myself for how you felt. Will you please forgive me for what I did and the hurt it caused you?" Jeeva asked.
> "Yes. I forgive you," I replied.
> "I promise never to do or say anything that will put you down in front of others from now on. I promise only to say positive and uplifting things about you. Is there any other change you would like me to make?" Jeeva added.
> "No, I'm happy with those changes," I responded.

Then hugs. And kisses. More hugs and more kisses. Rinse & repeat.

Please take note of the 5 elements of the process of reconciliation we followed, so you can apply them to your conflicts.

RESTORING PEACE FOLLOWING CONFLICT

1. **Take responsibility:**

    State exactly what you did that hurt your spouse. "I hurt you by…"

    Check with your spouse: "Did I get it right?" Change your statement of hurt according to their feedback. Do not question what they say (except for clarification). Do not justify or make excuses for what you did.

2. **Show empathy:**

    Make a sincere attempt to enter into your spouse's pain. Identify the feelings aroused by the hurt. Use the Feelings Chart, if necessary.

    Share with them the feelings you identified. "This is how you must have felt…"

    Check with your spouse for feedback on what you shared: "Did I identify all your feelings? Did I leave anything out?" Acknowledge any additional feelings they may share.

3. **Express remorse:**

    Share with them how you feel about hurting them. "I feel…"

4. **Request forgiveness:**

    "Will you please forgive me for what I did and the hurt it caused you?" Receive your spouse's forgiveness.

5. **Commit to change:**

    "These are the changes I will make to prevent this hurt from recurring." List them.

    Ask your spouse for feedback. "Is there any other change you would like me to make?" Agree to incorporate those changes into your commitment as well.

Action Step

> Now it is your turn. Make a list of all the hurts your spouse has caused you that remain unhealed. Use the Process of Reconciliation to receive your healing. For quick reference, you can access a printable PDF of this outline at www.thesams.ca/resources.

A PATTERN OF RESOLUTION

So far, we have received and released forgiveness (in the spirit realm) and gone through the steps of reconciliation (in the soul realm). We still need a plan to ensure that the hurt will not be repeated. This process is what we call Resolution (in the soul-body realm).

In the case of the cooking incident, the commitment to change was quite simple and acceptable to both parties. But there are times when it will take more than a couple of promises for the spouse who was hurt to be satisfied that their partner will not do it again.

Here are some common situations:
- One spouse keeps on spending money without any kind of accountability.
- One spends too much time pursuing their hobbies.
- Each of you have radically different ideas of how to spend your upcoming vacation.

In times like these, you could use a pattern such as this one.

Step 1: Meet In The Right Place...

Resolution is often blocked simply because you have attempted it at the wrong place. What might be an inappropriate place for conflict resolution? Anywhere others are present, such as a restaurant, family gathering or your home when the children are still up. Another place where you may not want to try resolving a conflict is when the two of you are in a vehicle. Why? Simply because neither one of you has the freedom to "leave the room" should things get too heated!

What might be a better place? Some space where you:
- Are guaranteed privacy.
- Feel secure and safe in bringing anything up.
- Have the freedom to take a break or call a time out.

Step 2: ... At The Right Time

Picking the right time to work on resolution is just as important. Here are some "wrong" times that will work against you:
- When your energy levels are low, e.g. at the end of a working day.
- When you are just sitting down for a meal.
- When you are physically exhausted.
- When you are mentally fatigued.
- When you are not feeling well.
- When you are on your period (for ladies only!)

You are much better off postponing the discussion to a time when you are both in a peaceful frame of mind and have the energy to talk through the issues clearly.

Step 3: Name The Issue You Are Resolving

Stick to the issue at hand. Address the offense without attacking the offender. Something focused like, "Let's talk about the kitchen being left messy at the end of the day," is preferable to, "Let's talk about how you can stop being a messy housekeeper." Focus on their behaviour, not their character. Deal with only one issue at a time. If you're talking about the kitchen, don't bring up the cluttered closet, the bathroom, the laundry room, or any other room. Avoid these words like the plague, "And while we're at it, what about …?" Keeping the focus on finding a solution to one particular issue speeds up the process considerably and promotes peaceful resolution.

> *Address the offense without attacking the offender.*

Step 4: Examine Yourself First Before Blaming The Other

Each of you must ask yourself, "How have I contributed to this problem, if at all?" and give an honest answer. This is a tricky step, because in most situations of conflict, we are prone to pinning the blame on our spouse. e.g. "You are the one who leaves the dishes in the sink for too long," or, "If only you weren't out with your friends all the time…"

It often appears that one person is totally responsible for the problem, but in our observation, this is rarely the case. For example, it may look like a husband is neglecting his wife and spending too much time with his buddies. However, if his wife is focused on her hobbies and not making time for him, he may feel rejected, which is why he spends time with his friends.

Let us be clear that each person is responsible for their own behaviour. Neither spouse should be let off the hook for their own actions. To properly address a recurring issue of conflict though, you need to take a high view that includes all contributing factors. This step is critical because we all have unmet needs, and much conflict arises simply from us trying to get our needs met. This also requires you to be humble, which is a good posture to have in general. Having said that, sometimes you may not be sure how you contributed to the hurt. Rather than taking a guess, simply ask your spouse, who we encourage to respond in a loving way with exactly what you did. Receive their response graciously.

Step 5: List All Possible Solutions Together

Notice the emphasis on the plural, solutions. Resolution is often not achieved because one spouse gets it in their head that there is only one way to solve this problem and they try to convince the other one to buy into it. There is always more than one solution to a problem. This is a time to brainstorm. Just keep on writing down whatever both your brains spit out as possible solutions. This is not the time to evaluate or dismiss any of them. Please make sure that both of you are providing your individual input in this step.

Step 6: Evaluate The Options & Agree On A Solution

Now that you have listed a few possible solutions, go back over them, one at a time. Share with each other the pros and cons that you can see for every solution. Cross off those that you know for certain will not work, at least not right now. Narrow down the workable choices until you are left with a few that genuinely have merit, like short-listing the applicants for a job. Pick one solution among the candidates that remain or create a hybrid of multiple solutions. Then agree on this single solution for the time being.

Give up any ownership rights to the solution that you choose. This solution now belongs to both of you equally, and rightfully so, because the two of you considered all possible solutions and agreed on one to try for now. Determine how long you will try it so that you have ample time to test its effectiveness.

Step 7: Follow Up And Evaluate

Set up another time to evaluate how the solution is working out. This meeting should be held after you have given your solution enough time. It could be after a week, a month, a couple of months or longer, depending on how long it takes to implement.

Share with each other how you are doing in keeping your end of the bargain. Is it working well for each of you? What difficulties, if any, are you encountering? What modifications, if any, would you suggest?

If, during this follow-up session, you conclude that the solution you chose is not working as well as you had hoped, fear not! Go back to Step 5 where you brainstormed and short-listed workable solutions and find another option to try out. Repeat Steps 6 and 7.

Step 8: Reward Each Other As You Make Progress

A reward does not have to be something that costs money. It could be as simple as a word of encouragement, "Hey, I notice you've been keeping your commitment to do the dishes right after dinner. That is awesome!" It could also be something tangible. Say you saved $300 by cutting down on eating out. Give yourself a $30 treat—pizza and wings or coffee and dessert.

If, after following this process, you are still not able to resolve your recurring issues of conflict, we encourage you to seek help from a qualified professional.

You may download a template of this pattern for to use as a worksheet at: www.thesams.ca/resources.

Before we move to the next segment of our Marriage Mentorship Process, let us help you seal the healing you have received so far with a ritual of reconciliation.

A RITUAL OF RECONCILIATION

Begin by reading aloud these words from 1 Corinthians 13:4–8a:

> *"Love is patient, love is kind. It does not envy, it does not boast, it is not proud. It does not dishonour others, it is not self-seeking, it is not easily angered, it keeps no record of wrongs. Love does not delight in evil but rejoices with the truth. It always protects, always trusts, always hopes, always perseveres. Love never fails."*

You will notice there are 15 attributes of love listed in these verses. Substitute "I" for "love," and read each attribute out loud. Ask yourself: Does it ring true for me? How much of the time? How would my spouse grade me on this aspect of love?

Using the following grid, rate yourself on a scale of 1–10 for each attribute, where 1 is "Rarely or Never," and 10 is "All the time."

	1	2	3	4	5	6	7	8	9	10
I am patient										
I am kind										
I do not envy										
I do not boast										
I am not proud										
I do not dishonour others										
I am not self-seeking										
I am not easily angered										
I keep no record of wrongs										
I do not delight in evil										
I rejoice with the truth										
I protect										
I trust										
I hope										
I persevere										

Ask God to forgive you for those attributes where you graded yourself at 5 or below. Ask your spouse to forgive you for those ways in which your failure to exhibit this characteristic of love has impacted them adversely. Be as specific as possible. Use the process of reconciliation as necessary.

Get a basin of warm water and a towel. Read John 13:1–15, where Jesus washes the feet of His disciples and tells them, *"Now that I, your Lord and Teacher, have washed your feet, you also should wash one another's feet."* Wash each other's feet—slowly, deliberately—as if to wash off the hurts that you confessed. Follow whatever directions the Holy Spirit gives you to experience and express that reconciliation.

Download pdfs of the Process of Reconciliation and the Pattern of Resolution at www.thesams.ca/resources or by scanning this QR code:

CHAPTER 7

GOING UNDERCOVERS

We have observed that a decline in sexual activity is often a tell-tale sign that something is not quite right in a marriage. Many couples who come to us for mentorship have not had sex for months, sometimes years. If this is you, there's hope! For most couples, there is nothing wrong physically; they are in good shape, with all the necessary apparatus in functioning mode, if you know what we mean! Yet sexual distancing has become the norm.

Do you ever find yourself saying any of the following things to your spouse when they hint at initiating a sexual connection?

> "Don't touch me!"
> "Just leave me alone. Can't you see I'm tired?"
> "You treat me like trash all day, and now you expect me to do what!?"
> "Don't interrupt me. Can't you see I'm watching this game?"

If so, it is worth examining why you feel this way, what has gone wrong in the relationship, and how to rebuild a lasting and enjoyable sexual connection.

THE ROOTS OF SEXUAL DISCONNECTION

Dom & Denise were connecting sexually from time to time, but neither was totally satisfied. As we started working with them, we discovered that they had a history of hurting one another by bringing up each other's mistakes from the past. Denise kept on reminding Dom about a poor business decision he had made several years earlier that affected their family's finances. Dom kept on re-hashing how she had alienated a close family friend with her words and actions.

Both readily admitted that what they kept doing to each other was wrong and had caused damage to their marriage. Denise was reluctant to respond to Dom's sexual advances in part because she had not received healing at the deepest possible level (spirit realm). She claimed to have forgiven him, but we discovered through conversation that she had not forgiven him for the effects of his decision upon her emotions and her thoughts (soul realm). As long as the effects of that hurt lingered, she was not ready to be intimate with him in a deep way.

Our healing team took her through a process where she identified the ways in which she was still holding on to emotional hurt and painful thoughts. She was able to forgive him from her heart. When she finally reached a place of healing, she was more willing to entertain the prospect of sexual intimacy.

Simultaneously, Dom identified the ways in which he was continuing to hurt her by blaming her over and over again for the alienation of their family friend. He acknowledged the negative impact of his actions upon Denise, including the feelings he had stirred up in her. He also received healing for his hurt in sessions with our team.

Once they were able to forgive each other and reach the point of reconciliation, they were also able to enjoy each other in a mutually satisfying sexual relationship.

See how the Spirit-Soul-Body Connection is at work in the Sexual Connection as well?

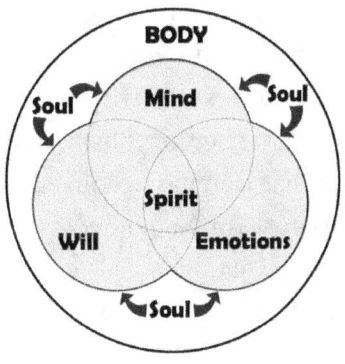

For things to change in the body realm, they first had to take care of their hurts in the spirit and the soul realms. You cannot resolve sexual issues in a marriage by beginning with the body. Sure, you can learn physical techniques or use stimulants to enhance your sexual performance. Granted these measures can make a difference, but only temporarily. You need to pay attention to your soul and your spirit as well.

Transparency & Emotional Connection

A second key factor that affects the sexual connection is the degree of transparency in your marriage. Here is a common list of trust matters that can cause either spouse to hold back sexually:

- withholding something financially
- battling an addiction that they are not willing to admit
- committing a sin they are not willing to confess
- hiding something from their past that they are ashamed of
- keeping any other kind of secret

Ken & Sue barely have sex anymore. She would like to, but he has been making excuses. He used to respond with such enthusiasm whenever she initiated the connection! She cannot understand why he is so different now. Sometimes he even snaps at her for "always" wanting sex. What Sue doesn't know is that Ken has become dependent on looking at pornography to get stimulated before engaging in sex. When he is not able to do that, he makes excuses about being tired or simply says that he is not up to it.

To resume a healthy sexual connection, Ken needs to come clean with Sue, knowing that she will likely be angry, disappointed, and even devastated when she finds out the truth. This transparency, while painful, will open the door to a path to healing and strengthen their emotional connection. He also needs to address the roots of his addiction to pornography with help from an expert in that area.

Emotional connection is affected not only by the withholding of past hurts or addictions, it is also often impacted by the tone of your daily interactions. Men often need to be reminded that when their wives feel emotionally distant from them, they are not able to connect sexually as freely as they might want to. On the other hand, when they feel emotionally close, women can often connect sexually with greater ease. That is not to say that men have no desire for an emotional connection with their wives, but in general, women tend to need that connection more.

A good clue that your spouse is trying to establish this emotional connection is when they start asking questions like: "How was your day? How are you feeling? Is anything bothering you? What are you going through?" Do not be put off by what seems like probing questions. Look at them as opportunities to strengthen your emotional connection. If you are struggling to respond with feeling words, pull out the Feeling Chart and speak the emotional language that your spouse longs to hear from you.

Sexual intimacy typically flows out of emotional intimacy, which begins with transparency.

In any event, and for either gender, pay attention to your spouse's desire for emotional intimacy. Sexual intimacy typically flows out of emotional intimacy, which begins with transparency. When you get close to each other emotionally, you are also able to enjoy physical intimacy in a way that is fulfilling to both of you.

The Oxytocin Factor

A third factor that affects the sexual connection is neither spiritual nor emotional, but physical. It is a powerful hormone called oxytocin, responsible for such diverse functions as contractions during labour, releasing milk while breastfeeding and promoting bonding between a mother and her baby. Oxytocin also promotes connection between a husband and a wife, as it is responsible for sexual arousal and orgasm. It is often described as the "connection chemical" or the "bonding hormone." Physical touch of all kinds, including simple platonic touch between friends, triggers oxytocin. While oxytocin levels typically remain high for women, male levels come close to matching females only during orgasm.[14]

Ever since I (Sulojana) became aware of the oxytocin factor, I have been more sensitive to Jeeva's need for sexual connection. I now realize that when he expresses his craving for sex, he is not being an animal, he just really wants to bond with me. He is longing to experience not only the emotional intimacy of sex, but also the connection that comes with the oxytocin rush.

At the same time, men need to recognize that this craving for the oxytocin rush does not give them permission to demand sex from their wife, ever. She has to be willing and ready to entertain the sexual connection. It must always be by mutual consent that couples have sex.

---

[14] Dr. Michael Gurian. *What Could He Be Thinking?: How a Man's Mind Really Works.*

Mutuality Is Key

Christian men need to be particularly careful not to abuse Scriptures such as Paul's teachings in 1 Corinthians 7 to "prove" that you can demand sex whenever you want it. Tragically, this has been commonplace in many "Christian" marriages.

> *"The husband should fulfill his marital duty to his wife, and likewise the wife to her husband. The wife does not have authority over her own body but yields it to her husband. In the same way, the husband does not have authority over his own body but yields it to his wife"* (1 Corinthians 7:3–4).

Pay attention to the mutuality that is woven throughout this passage.

> "The husband should fulfill... and likewise the wife."
> "The wife does not have authority over her own body... the husband does not have authority over his own body."
> "The wife yields it to her husband... the husband yields it to his wife."

Whatever is spoken of the husband is equally applicable to the wife, and vice versa. In voluntarily yielding authority over their bodies to each other, a husband and a wife mirror Jesus, who voluntarily yielded His privileged position as a member of the Godhead to become human (Philippians 2:6–7). Yielding authority over your body to your spouse is a voluntary act of giving. Having authority over your spouse's body is not a right but a gift. Paul is not giving blanket permission for a husband to demand sex from his wife anytime he wants to or vice versa. You need to ensure that your spouse is freely giving their body voluntarily and not out of compulsion, obligation or a sense of duty.

> Paul goes on to say: *"Do not deprive each other except perhaps by mutual consent and for a time, so that you may devote yourselves to prayer. Then come together again so that Satan will not tempt you because of your lack of self-control. I say this as a concession, not as a command"* (1 Corinthians 7:5–6).

Depriving each other of sex is only by "mutual consent." This means that the consent of both parties is required to abstain from sexual relations. Does this mean that when one does not consent, the other one can still have their way with their spouse? Not at all. That would qualify as sexual abuse and rape.

> **A sexless marriage is not part of God's design**

Having said that, we also need to pay attention to the word "deprive." The Greek word translated "deprive" literally means "to rob" or "to defraud." In other words, enjoying sexual connection is the expected norm in marriage. Depriving each other is not the norm. A sexless marriage is not part of God's design. Therefore, Paul goes on to say that such depriving is meant to last "for a time" and only "that you may devote yourselves to prayer." After such a period, "you should come together again." Abstinence is temporary only. Why is this so important? Paul warns husbands and wives of a serious consequence of prolonged abstinence for even the noblest of reasons, such as prayer. It could be used by the enemy to tempt both husband and wife, if there is also a lack of self-control.

Not having sex can open the door for Satan to tempt you, where you might give in to fantasy, pornography, or the sexual advances of another person. However, and we state this emphatically, how you deal with temptation is *your* responsibility, not your spouse's. A Holy Spirit-led person should not give in to such temptation. Lack of sex in a marriage is no excuse for you to turn to other outlets for sex or to seek out opportunities for intimacy that you are not finding at home. You need to exercise self-control (a fruit of the spirit, according to Galatians 5:23). These words from Paul offer encouragement:

> *"No temptation has overtaken you except what is common to humankind. And God is faithful; he will not let you be tempted beyond what you can bear. But when you are tempted, he will also provide a way out so that you can endure it"* (1 Corinthians 10:13).

Jude reminds us that we have a *"God who is able to keep you from falling into sin"* (Jude 1:24). You can endure temptation and emerge faithfully victorious. At the same time, if lack of sexual connection is contributing to your temptation, you both need to find out how your marriage got to this place.

IMPROVING YOUR SEXUAL CONNECTION

Following are a few practical considerations to work through for increased sexual intimacy. By making a few changes, you should be able to move your sexual relationship from bust to robust. If you are finding it difficult to achieve sexual satisfaction in your marriage with mutuality, please seek professional sexual counselling.

Affection And Appreciation Outside The Bedroom

You need to be aware of how affection in the open affects passion under the covers. Take a moment to think about all the interactions you have as husband and wife outside the bedroom. Some of these interactions involve talking. If you were to keep track of all the times that you talk to each other…

- How much of your talk is affectionate?
- How much would be classified under one of the "4 C's" (Criticizing, Condemning, Complaining and Comparing)?
- Would there be words that qualify as put-downs, defamation, calling each other unflattering names?
- Would there be words that make your spouse feel sexy, admired, appreciated?
- How much would be simply conveying information?
- How much would be "giving orders" or more "to-do list" type talk?

In other words, if the only time you tell your spouse that you find them attractive is when you are trying to seduce them, or if you are calling them all sorts of unloving names during the day and then telling them "Oh, I love you, baby!" because you want to have sex, you are not likely to have a great sexual relationship. You can't treat your spouse like dirt outside the bedroom and expect them to treat you like gold in bed.

Instead, decide to appreciate your spouse for all that they do during the day. Express your affection at every available opportunity—with words of appreciation, touches, caresses, hugs, love notes in their lunch box or on the pillow, lipstick on the bathroom mirror—let your creativity run wild! Let your spouse know beyond a shadow of a doubt that you not only love them, but also genuinely like them, delight in them, cherish them, celebrate them, and adore them. This is more likely to lead both of you to connect sexually in a natural way.

> *You can't treat your spouse like dirt outside the bedroom and expect them to treat you like gold in bed.*

You can learn a lot about expressing affection and appreciation from Song of Solomon in the Bible. The book opens with these words spoken by the wife:

> *"My beloved is to me a sachet of myrrh resting between my breasts. My beloved is to me a cluster of henna blossoms from the vineyards of En Gedi…How handsome you are, my beloved! Oh, how charming! And our bed is verdant"* (Song of Solomon 1:13–14, 16).

Listen to his responses:

> "How beautiful are your sandaled feet, princess! The curves of your thighs are like jewelry, the handiwork of a master. Your navel is a rounded bowl; it never lacks mixed wine. Your waist is a mound of wheat surrounded by lilies. Your breasts are like two fawns, twins of a gazelle... How beautiful you are and how pleasant, my love, with such delights!" (Song of Solomon 7:1–3, 6)

Not all of us will be quite as poetic or artistic in painting vivid word pictures when we express our affection and appreciation to our spouse. Let the words of your mouth come from the depths of your heart. Never downplay the power they carry. They act as verbal foreplay that sets the stage for a fulfilling sexual connection.

Ongoing Communication

You need to communicate with each other about which aspects of your sexual relationship are pleasing to you and which are not. This is especially important if you have had sexual relationships with anyone other than your spouse. You can operate with certain assumptions about what is good and pleasurable based on those previous experiences, and cause great harm to each other.

The more openly you communicate with each other the better. Let your spouse know:

- What kind of touching is pleasurable for you? What is not?

- Are you experiencing any pain or discomfort during sexual intercourse?
- Is your partner being too rough? Or could they be more emphatic?
- What other forms of sexual expression are you open to? What is unacceptable for you?

If you do not tell them, they could keep on hurting you without even being aware that they are. We have seen couples in our Marriage Mentorship Process shock each other by sharing how a certain sexual practice that their partner thought was perfectly normal was totally repugnant to the other one, but they had never expressed this. Speak up, people!

If it is not mutually acceptable, it is not permissible.

Remember the principle of mutual consent. Whatever sexual practice you are considering, if it is not mutually acceptable, it is not permissible. If it pleasurable to both of you and is hurting no one, let mutuality be your guide. This applies to oral sex, toys and any other kinds of sexual pleasure that you can think of.

If one or both partners has experienced sexual hurt in the past, including abuse or assault, and memories of these events interrupt or inhibit sex with your spouse, we encourage you to communicate about this. Please also seek out and receive the healing you need, so that the injustices of your past do not rob your future of joy and fun.

Performance Anxiety

Most depictions of sexual activity, especially in movies and on TV, create unhealthy expectations of sex in marriage. For the most part, so-called "love scenes" are marked by extraordinary expressions of passion. Editing techniques make sexual encounters seem as though they took just a couple of minutes from start to finish. Many times "TV sex" culminates in a climactic orgasm, accompanied by heavy breathing, seductive moaning or even screaming, not to mention a soundtrack that amplifies the intensity of the experience. Almost always they end with a shot of the exhausted couple lying there with an unmistakable look of satisfaction on their faces.

We are given the impression that this is "normal" for a couple having sex. In reality, this is fiction. If you expect the earth to shake and fireworks to go off with loud orchestral music rising to a crescendo every time you have sex, you may be in for some disappointment. Any time you place such an expectation on yourself or your spouse, you are creating "orgasmic pressure" and fostering unhelpful performance anxiety.

When someone has been exposed to pornography, even more unrealistic expectations are imprinted upon their brain. In contrast to movie scenes which make the sexual encounter appear short, pornography gives the impression that they go on forever. This often puts pressure on the husband to have incredible stamina. When these expectations do not pan out, he could suffer a terrible letdown. He begins to wonder: "What's wrong with me?" Even worse, he starts blaming his wife, "What's wrong with you?" Similarly, when a wife expects her husband to make her orgasm everytime—as she has seen repeatedly on the screen—and this doesn't happen, she can end up being greatly disappointed.

Sex under such self-imposed stress is not likely to be satisfying. The sad fact of the matter is that the culprit behind this stress is unrealistic expectations. When you set your expectations aright, you can avoid this altogether. Instead of subjecting yourself to "orgasmic pressure", what you really should be aiming for is "organic pleasure." This is pleasure that comes simply from enjoying each other physically—whether it is only kisses and sweet caresses, fondling and sensual massages or sexual intercourse. Simply focus on enjoying each other intimately, whether it leads to an orgasm or not.

Physical Considerations

A final consideration is the physical factors that influence sex. Let us say at the outset that you should not feel compelled or forced to attain an ideal body weight, shape, or condition simply for the sake of pleasing your partner sexually. There is absolutely no room for body-shaming or fat-shaming in a Christ-centered marriage.

While achieving a certain size or shape should not be your focus, paying attention to health and strength is an asset to sexual fulfilment. We will do well to heed these words by Emily Nagoski, from her book *Come As You Are*: "We are all the same. We are all different. We are all normal."

There are three physical considerations that we would like to place before you.

Fitness

Studies have shown a correlation between our level of physical fitness and our ability to fully enjoy each other sexually.[15] This has to do with the fact that our energy levels are higher when we exercise regularly. Higher energy levels also increase our stamina which in turn has an impact on our endurance levels while we are having sex.

It is also true that when one spouse or both have excessive belly fat, penetration can be difficult or even impossible. One spouse's weight can also be a burden for the other spouse to bear. These factors could diminish the measure of pleasure you experience.

We both do our very best to make sure that we are physically fit. We take walks together whenever the weather permits. In addition, Jeeva prefers to do high intensity interval training, so he will go for a combination walk and run on his own. Sulojana favours the elliptical in the house. We also eat as healthily as possible. Regardless of what you do and how you do it, please ensure that you are doing your very best to stay physically fit.

Personal hygiene

There are no universal standards that govern this area. If you prefer your spouse to smell as paleo as possible, that is your standard. If your spouse asks you to brush your teeth, use mouthwash, floss, take a quick shower with body wash of a particular scent, apply deodorant to your armpits and wear a

---

[15] https://www.ncbi.nlm.nih.gov/pmc/articles/PMC5963213/

certain cologne or perfume, then that is what you should do. Regardless of what you do, please make sure that you are honouring your spouse's preferences in this area and not repelling them by poor hygiene.

Health issues

Take care of all health issues that could affect your sex life. Diabetes, heart and vascular disease, depression, chronic pain, erectile dysfunction, and migraines are some conditions that are known to be factors in sexual dysfunction. Please get the treatment and care that you need. We also need to acknowledge that some conditions may continue to affect you, despite your best efforts to address them medically. Sometimes, certain medications and treatments that are prescribed could also have an impact on your libido. As a couple, you need to be sensitive to each other's needs in this area and love them "in sickness and in health" as you pledged in your wedding vows.

THE PLAGUE OF PORNOGRAPHY

Pornography is a major factor affecting marriages, including Christian marriages. According to a survey by Proven Men, the number of Christian men viewing pornography nearly mirrors the national average in the United States: 97% have viewed pornography, 64% view porn at least once a month, 37% look at porn several times a week and 65% reported watching pornography at work.[16]

---

[16] https://www.provenmen.org/pornography-survey-statistics-2014/

The authors of *The Great Sex Rescue* also found that 13% of Christian married women report ever having used pornography and 3.7% report using it regularly or in intermittent binges.[17] A 2016 Barna report called The Porn Phenomenon[18] revealed that 57% of pastors and 64% of youth pastors admit they have struggled with porn and 21% of youth pastors and 14% of pastors admit they currently struggle with using porn.

I (Jeeva) can relate. I have struggled with it myself. I would give in to the temptation to watch sexually suggestive or explicit scenes when I was by myself in a hotel room, for example. And then I would feel awful about what I had just done.

Our son Sathiya, founder of DeepClean (a proven process which helps men get freedom from porn addiction) puts it this way: "When you are hungry, eating McDonalds is a way to meet your need for food. Is it healthy? No. Did it meet the need? Yes, for about 20 minutes if you ate their chicken, and about 12 minutes if you ate their beef. Pornography is the same for your soul. If you've struggled with porn, you will know that while watching pornography is exhilarating in the moment, it is anything but rewarding afterwards. Feelings of guilt, shame and disgust are quick to follow these experiences."

---

[17] Sheila Wray Gregoire et al. *The Great Sex Rescue*.

[18] https://www.barna.com/the-porn-phenomenon/

I (Jeeva) say a loud amen to that. Thankfully, my occasional consumption never grew into a daily addiction. But because I was so caught up in my own guilty pleasure, I never gave any thought to the impact my selfishness would have on Sulojana.

When Jeeva finally had the courage to share his struggle with me (Sulojana), I was totally devastated. The embarrassment and shame I experienced was unbearable. I felt as though he had been cheating on me. Even though porn is often seen as "emotional" adultery, as far as I was concerned, he might as well have had sexual encounters with multiple partners. No wonder Jesus says that *"anyone who looks at a woman lustfully has already committed adultery with her in his heart"* (Matthew 5:28b). I began to lose respect for him as the spiritual head of our home, until he started making positive changes.

The Harmful Effects Of Porn

Studies show that partners of those who use porn report that their self-esteem, relationship quality and sexual satisfaction are affected negatively. They also show that men who use porn regularly are more likely to suffer from erectile dysfunction, premature ejaculation, and delayed ejaculation, all of which increase with ongoing porn use.[19]

---

[19] https://fightthenewdrug.org/how-porn-can-negatively-impact-love-and-intimacy/

In "An Open Letter on Porn,"[20] respected relationship experts Drs. John & Julie Gottman list some of the effects of porn on a marriage. Here are a few:

- "Normal sex" becomes much less interesting for porn users.
- Use of pornography by one partner leads the couple to have far less sex and ultimately reduces relationship satisfaction.
- When watching pornography, the user is in total control of the sexual experience, in contrast to normal sex in which people are sharing control with the partner. Thus, a porn user may form the unrealistic expectation that sex will be under only one person's control.
- The porn user may expect that their partner will always be immediately ready for intercourse. This is unrealistic as well.
- Worse still, many porn sites include images and video of violence toward women, the antithesis of intimate connection.
- Pornography can also lead to a decrease in relationship trust and a higher likelihood of affairs outside the relationship.

Wives have reported on occasion that their husbands expect them to participate in acts that push them outside their comfort zone. Men who are exposed to such images believe these acts are normal and end up inflicting violence upon their

---

[20] https://www.gottman.com/blog/an-open-letter-on-porn/

wives, all the while expecting them to respond with pleasure. This is totally unacceptable.

Sheila Wray Gregoire also points out that "One of the problems with porn or erotica use is that it pairs sexual arousal and response with external stimuli rather than with your spouse. People often then dissociate by fantasizing or pulling up images in their minds to become aroused when they are with their spouse."[21]

Another significant way that porn affects intimacy in a marriage is by reducing transparency. According to a survey by Proven Men,[22] 25% of men and 20% of women say they have erased their internet browsing history in the last 30 days in order to hide or conceal their viewing of pornography or other sexually explicit content. Since what remains concealed cannot be healed, consumers of porn carry on their lives with a lack of transparency that impacts the level of intimacy with their spouse. This in turn leads to erosion of trust.

Unfortunately, many tolerate viewing porn as a "harmless" pastime. Some even consider it helpful. Some couples believe that watching porn together strengthens their sexual connection. Research proves the exact opposite. According to a study,[23] individuals who watched porn alone reported twice

---

[21] Sheila Wray Gregoire et al. *The Great Sex Rescue.*

[22] https://www.provenmen.org/pornography-survey-statistics-2014/

[23] Maddox, A. M., Rhoades, G. K., & Markman, H. J. (2011). Viewing Sexually-Explicit Materials Alone Or Together: Associations With Relationship Quality. Archives Of Sexual Behavior, 40(2), 441–448

the rate of cheating on their partner in comparison to couples who didn't watch porn at all. And interestingly, individuals who viewed porn alone and with their partners reported three times the rate of cheating.

Very clearly, pornography distorts the nature of a truly intimate sexual connection marked by mutual consent (1 Corinthians 7) and organic pleasure and has the potential to destroy your marriage. We fully agree with Sheila Wray Gregoire when she says: "Porn is not relational, mutual, or loving—it is degrading, violent and purely carnal."[24]

> *Pornography distorts the nature of a truly intimate sexual connection... and has the potential to destroy your marriage.*

Freedom From Porn

As Christians, we are called to do all in our power to *"flee from sexual immorality"* (1 Corinthians 6:18). It is beyond the scope of this book to provide detailed steps you can take to be set free from the bondage of pornography, however, we can share some simple steps that may help.

My (Jeeva's) road to recovery has taken me through inner healing sessions, deliverance ministry, seeking accountability and establishing healthy boundaries. I have learned to H.A.L.T

---

[24] Sheila Wray Gregoire et al. *The Great Sex Rescue.*

lustful thoughts and call on the power of the Holy Spirit when I feel too weak to resist temptation, thus ensuring that even those periodic episodes of consuming porn are a distant memory. Sulojana and I made a pact that anytime I allow a lustful thought to linger and slip into a fantasy, I will confess it to her. We have also found that making love with eyes open and soft lighting in the room keeps me from dissociating.

Jeeva's transparency has contributed to an increase in our intimacy. He installed an internet filtering software at my (Sulojana's) request. This way he is alerted about sites that contain sexual content if he lands on one unintentionally. Since I am notified of violations, we can have conversations about such temptations and how he responded to them. He also took my suggestion to join an accountability group. As painful as it was when I first heard about it, I have worked through that pain and found the grace to forgive him. I am now able to trust that he is not seeking refuge in pornography anymore and respect him. I do my part to help him stay free.

If pornography has infected your marriage and impacted your intimacy, please do not wait another moment to seek and receive the help you need. You may need to invest time and money connecting with someone who can help. Please reach out to one or more of the resources we have listed at the end of this book. There is hope for you. There is help for you. Healing awaits you.

GUIDELINES FOR SEXUAL CONNECTION

Based on all these considerations, here are some guidelines that we have established for our marriage that you are welcome to use.

- Prioritize sex in your schedule. Even write it into your calendar, if you need to. The same time, every week, has worked for us. We recognize this is a lot easier to do for some than others. Also, during certain seasons of life, such as when you have a baby or young children, it is not as easy. Those whose children are older and empty nesters like us would find it easier. Regardless, we highly recommend that you do your very best to have one set time a week and honour it. On that set day, make sure that you are both rested up and complete all your chores well in advance, so that nothing can stand in the way of you enjoying each other and focusing totally on each other. Let it be something you can look forward to, even in the midst of all your busyness.
- Allow room for spontaneity. Just in case you got the impression that scheduling a set time for sex would put the brakes on spontaneity, relax! We have good news for you! You are not limited to just one scheduled episode per week (we heard your big sigh of relief!). You can have as much sex as you like. Let the Spirit lead you and let friskiness bubble up!
- Connect emotionally with each other more frequently than you connect sexually. This means that you must make room every day for times to check in with your

spouse to see how they are feeling. If this is a new routine for you, you may need to set aside specific times every week on your calendar simply for emotional connection. For starters, try two times as much emotional connection as sexual connection. As we mentioned earlier, lack of emotional connection can be more of a roadblock for women than men. Marriage experts Barry & Lori Byrne recommend that husbands take the lead in initiating emotional connection while wives take the lead in initiating the physical connection. Once again, we recognize that this may not apply to all, as some husbands crave emotional connection more than their wives. In either case, it would be good for you to let your spouse know that you need to connect more emotionally. Then show them how to keep your emotional love tank full.
- Connect physically every day with gestures of affection that do not necessarily lead to sex, such as hugs, kisses, caresses, sensual touch, or whatever else your spouse enjoys.
- Remove all hindrances standing in the way of you giving yourselves to each other, before you initiate the sexual connection. Come clean with any temptations you did not resist, e.g. pornography, fantasy, lust. Let your spouse know of any hurt they have caused you that has not been addressed yet. Take responsibility for any hurt you know you caused them or whatever they point out to you. Go through the steps for restoring the peace as necessary. We find ourselves using the process of reconciliation regularly.

- Prepare yourselves as best as you can physically so you can give yourselves to each other unreservedly. Eat healthy foods, exercise regularly, take care of health issues and maintain the standard of personal hygiene your spouse expects of you.

GOD WANTS YOU TO ENJOY SEX

Let us conclude this chapter by reminding you that God wants us all to enjoy the pleasure and benefits of sexual connection with our spouse.

Look at these verses from Song of Solomon where the husband says:

> *Your stature is like that of the palm, and your breasts like clusters of fruit. I said, "I will climb the palm tree; I will take hold of its fruit." May your breasts be like clusters of grapes on the vine, the fragrance of your breath like apples, and your mouth like the best wine* (Song of Solomon 7:7–9a).

Is there any mistaking what he means by climbing the palm tree?

The wife responds:

> *"May the wine go straight to my beloved, flowing gently over lips and teeth. I belong to my beloved, and his desire is for me. Come, my beloved, let us go to the countryside let us spend the night in the villages. Let us go early to the vineyards to see if*

the vines have budded, if their blossoms have opened, and if the pomegranates are in bloom—there I will give you my love" (Song of Solomon 7:9b–12).

They are both unabashed in expressing their desire to experience sexual intimacy with one another. So should you, dear husband and wife. This is why God designed you the way He did and planted this desire in you. The fact that such sexually descriptive verses are in the Bible leaves no doubt about God's will for mutually-pleasurable sex.

Action Steps

1. Share with each other what the Holy Spirit highlighted for you in this chapter. Be vulnerable and transparent.

2. What are some steps you need to take today to improve your sexual connection?

For additional discussion questions on this chapter, go to www.thesams.ca/resources or scan the QR code below:

CHAPTER 8

MAKING TIME

We often hear couples say: "We just don't have enough time for each other." The reality is that all of us have 24 hours in a day (minus sleep time). The issue is not that you do not have enough time; it is that you are not making enough time to be with each other. In other words, you need to be intentional about making time for each other. It does not happen by accident.

> *One of the reasons why making time is so important is because it lets your spouse know that you value them.*

One of the reasons why making time is so important is because it lets your spouse know that you value them. Let's face it, we spend time on whatever we value and with those we value, right?

Many years ago, we heard a very wealthy business owner share his secret to building a multi-billion-dollar business without sacrificing his marriage and his family on the altar of success. He said: "I learned to make time for my business around my family commitments." That is the exact opposite of the way most people do it, is it not?

> *Our calendar reflects our priority to make time for the one who matters the most to us.*

We cannot say that we were always successful in accomplishing this, but we do our best to ensure that our calendar reflects our priority to make time for the one who matters the most to us. Here are some things we have done over the years that have helped us to make time for each other.

A Common Calendar

We have a common calendar on the kitchen wall where we both mark down everything that is going on in our lives—appointments, events, meetings, phone calls with family, exercise—everything. This helps us avoid unnecessary conflict that can arise from double-booking. You can just as easily achieve this with an electronic calendar; it is just that we prefer the paper variety. As a bonus, if you have grown children at home, it helps them know what Mom and Dad are up to as well.

Our Night A Week

We set aside a stretch of time every week for us to be together as a couple. We observe it religiously. Some call it "Date Night," we simply consider it "Our Night." You can call it whatever you like, but the main thing is that you have a block of time set apart just for the two of you to be together, to enjoy each other's company, to do something fun. Intimacy expert Monica Tanner recommends a minimum of 3 hours of uninterrupted time.

We are asked sometimes how a couple with young children can do this consistently. If possible, you could wait till they go to bed and take some time just for the two of you. Wherever possible, we highly recommend making childcare arrangements, to ensure that you have your time together. If you are blessed to have grandparents or other close family near you, caring for your children a few hours a week could be a gift they give you. If you have close friends with children who also need a block of time to be together, you could take turns looking after each other's children and make it work for both couples. If such arrangements are not possible, see how you can work it into your budget.

In case you are worried about the cost of "Our Night," let us assure you that you can make this happen without breaking the bank.

What do we do on "Our Night?"

We may occasionally go out for coffee or sometimes for a meal, but that is not what we do most of the time. Mostly, we stay home! We may work on a jigsaw puzzle together, or watch an episode of a TV series, a movie or some other favourite show (with popcorn, of course!). We prefer funny or romantic shows, but you pick whatever you will both enjoy. Play a card game you enjoy or your favourite board game. Play in a way that is relaxing and enjoyable. If you must be competitive, remember to be kind! If you would rather do something physically active, go for a bike ride or put on your snowshoes in the winter and blaze a trail! Go to the gym or go for a run or a skate.

The main message you are sending each other is: "I like being with you. I want to be with you. I want you to know that you are important to me."

Exceptions to the weekly rule

You may be asking: "What if we cannot schedule the same time every week, because we work shifts, we are on call, etc.?" We admit that may be tricky, but you can always come up with a way to make it work. For example, you could take a half day off together every two weeks or a full day once a month. Or go away for a weekend every few months. You need to have an oasis in the distance that you can look forward to in the midst of all the demands of life on your time and energy.

Time Together And Apart From Each Other

You not only need to work at spending time together, but also at spending time apart from each other—pursuing hobbies, leisure, and sporting activities that you enjoy by yourself without your spouse actively participating with you. In short, you need to make the time to do what is important for each of you.

For example, he loves to play recreational hockey and she reaches for a winter jacket when the temperature drops below 22 degrees Celsius (70 F). In other words, there is no way she is going to be cheering him on in the ice-cold rink, because that is not her preference. Or maybe her interest is bowling and he is no alley cat! One way to accommodate these different interests is to schedule both activities on the same night. If he is happy freezing himself at the hockey arena, then she can be jolly sweating it out at the bowling alley. Both get to enjoy their time apart. Hallelujah! When Jeeva had meetings at the church, those were Sulojana's nights to go out for coffee with friends, or simply stay home and read. What you need to make sure is that you have time together, as well as time apart, so that you can pursue the things you want to do together as well as the activities you prefer to do on your own.

Plan Your Week Together

The other important thing is to plan your week together. Yes, we have the monthly calendar, but we also look at that calendar and see what is happening that week. Taking that "week at a glance" really helps avoid any scheduling conflicts. We do this on Sunday evenings. We look at the week ahead and make sure that all our appointments are on the calendar. Then we pray into them. We also check to see that our week includes time for us to be together and time apart from each other. Those of you with children need to make sure that you make enough time to be with them also.

At the beginning of each day, we take a minute or two to make sure that we are clear about what each other is doing that day. This way we will catch any unexpected changes that may not have been added to our common calendar.

At the end of the day, we have a quick chat about what happened during the day:

> "Hey, how was your day?"
> "How did that meeting go with so-and-so?"
> "How was that dental appointment?"
> "Anything else that I need to be aware of that happened today?"

The key once again is that we are making time to check in with each other. These are not long chats, just very quick conversations. For us, these touch points often take place in the car—on our drive to work and back. Or at breakfast in the morning and at dinner in the evening. At the end of the day, we thank God for everything we accomplished that day. Then we talk about what is on the calendar for the following day and pray into those commitments as well before we go to bed.

The fact is, if you do not make time for each other, you will end up giving each other what is left over after you have given the best of yourself to everyone else. You can get by with leftovers from time to time, but you cannot live on them. Routines get stale, and you are bound to get frustrated when you do not feel valued. Here are some practical steps you can take to make time for each other.

Action Steps

1. Look at your calendar for this month.
2. Set aside weekly blocks of uninterrupted time to be together first (minimum 3 hours, if possible).
3. Block off all children's activities that require your presence (if any).
4. Mark all your working hours/scheduled business time slots.
5. Block off time for exercise, sleep and periods of rest.
6. Enter your time apart to pursue your individual interests/hobbies.
7. Go back and make any adjustments required to ensure that your calendar reflects your priorities.
8. Decide together what you will do with the rest of the available free time (if any).

By following these steps, you will make sure that you are making time in your marriage for the people who matter the most to you, beginning with each other.

CHAPTER 9

MARITAL FINANCES

Finances are often cited as a major cause of marital stress which could contribute to the breakdown of a marriage. According to Dave Ramsay, this often happens when one spouse is a "saver" and the other a "spender." This was true of us (as you will soon find out) and of most couples we have mentored as well. We have also discovered that there are a host of factors that are responsible for moulding us into one or the other. In this chapter, we will identify these factors and share several other causes of financial stress in a marriage.

As you go through the rest of this chapter, put a check mark beside those that are a source of stress in your marriage right now. This way you can see which of our guidelines can help you address them and even eliminate them for good.

KEY CAUSES OF FINANCIAL STRESS

Different Philosophies

This is a factor that contributed to financial stress in our marriage. Both our families had very different philosophies about how to handle financial matters.

Sulojana's dad was a strong believer that you should have every last penny saved before you make a purchase—and that applied to everything from clothes for the kids to buying a house. In those days, this was quite a common thought process among most people in India. He could not stand the thought of paying interest.

Jeeva's parents were not that stringent about saving up before buying, even though they too were raised in India. They were more than happy to take a loan for certain purchases, as long as they had a game plan and the cash flow to take care of the payments. Once I (Jeeva) started working, the local bank was only too eager to lend me money for just about anything I wanted to buy. Within a matter of months, I had already built up quite an impressive portfolio—of debt! I had a student loan, a car loan and a credit card balance on which I was making minimum monthly payments.

Shortly after Sulojana came to Canada, I wanted us to buy a house. Sulojana asked me, "Where is the money for the house coming from? Have you saved it all up?" That's when I told her that the Canadian way of buying a house is to get a mortgage. All we needed to do was to find a bank that would lend us what we needed, and we were all set. Needless to say, she was mortified! I also conveniently forgot to tell her that *mortgage* literally translates to "death grip," but she went along with my plan anyway, though very reluctantly.

If you are facing financial stress in your marriage, could it be because you were raised with different financial philosophies in your family of origin?

Established Patterns

A second source of financial stress is a result of the unique patterns both of you had already established before you got married. This is becoming more of a factor now as the average age at which couples get married goes steadily up. We have met couples where one spouse would keep track of where every penny came from and went, while the other was, shall we say, more relaxed about it. They get married and the "accountant" spouse asks the "free spirit" spouse for details of where they are spending the money.

> "What do you mean I need to show you where all *my* money has been going? You're not trying to tell me how I should spend *my* money, are you?"
> "Not at all. I'm trying to do what is best for our family. If we want to save up for a house, we need to know exactly how much we need for expenses, so we can figure out how much we can put away, right?"
> "You make it sound good, but I feel like you're trying to control *my* spending."
> "No, I'm not trying to control you, dear, *you* are being reckless with *our* money."

In this example, the stress actually has very little to do with the money itself. The problem arose because of ingrained habits, which by themselves are not problematic, they're just different. It is possible that this couple's patterns came from what they saw their parents do, or what they learned from friends, books or seminars.

When a man and a woman with their own established patterns couple up, they could generate much stress. Recognizing the differences in these embedded patterns is the first step in ensuring that such discussions do not sabotage their marriage.

Do you recognize any such patterns in your marriage?

Underlying Beliefs

These are beliefs that we usually learn from our parents. You often do not even realize that they are part of your belief system, simply because you heard someone say them repeatedly. Here are some we have heard over the years:

> "Do you think money grows on trees?"
> "You never want to be rich... look at all the problems rich people have!"
> "There is only so much to go around."
> "Money is the root of all evil." (This is a common misquote of 1 Timothy 6:10, which actually says: *"The love of money is a root of all kinds of evil"*).

One belief that I (Jeeva) had developed came out of a statement that I heard my Mom make over and over again during my growing-up years: "God will never give us more than we need." She intended to say that God would always provide us with all that we needed and that we would never lack. But the way it was phrased had an unintended impact upon me: I internalized it to believe that I would never experience abundance. Therefore, I could never be comfortable with having more than what was sufficient to meet our essential needs.

Even worse, my mind kept on prompting me to take measures which ensured that we never had a surplus. I would quickly spend any extra income on something or give it away to someone, or worse, get into debt (which I will share in more detail later in this chapter). All because I was acting out of an underlying belief that God never wanted me to have more than enough to meet our needs.

In an inner healing session, I identified this thought pattern and forgave my Mom for contributing to the unbiblical belief I had developed. Then I replaced this unhealthy (and ungodly) belief with truth from Scripture, in verses such as:

> *"And God is able to bless you abundantly, so that in all things at all times, having all that you need, you will abound in every good work… You will be enriched in every way so that you can be generous on every occasion…"* (2 Corinthians 9:8, 11).
>
> *"Let the Lord be magnified, who has pleasure in the prosperity of His servant"* (Psalm 35:27 NKJV).

> *"The Lord will send a blessing on your barns and on everything you put your hand to…The Lord will grant you abundant prosperity—in the fruit of your womb, the young of your livestock and the crops of your ground—in the land he swore to your ancestors to give you"* (Deuteronomy 28:8a, 11).

Once I received the healing I needed and aligned my mindset with God's, that ungodly belief could no longer survive. A hindrance to experiencing financial wholeness was removed.

Can you identify any underlying beliefs you may be holding?

Not Having Enough Income

Financial stress can be a reality when there is not enough money coming in to meet your expenses. The effect is similar when you experience a job loss, a business failure or an unexpected medical or other expense that wipes you out.

There are pre-emptive measures you can take to help reduce the likelihood of such unexpected events from impacting your finances, such as always having 3–6 months' worth of expenses in a savings account. You can also take proactive measures to reduce or eliminate this stress, such as starting a side hustle or a home-based business, providing services (housecleaning, yard work, childcare, consulting, an array of online services, etc.). Do your best to be creative in finding something that works for you.

If not having enough income is an issue for you, what can you do right now to address it?

Debts

We live in a society where debt is an accepted fact of life. Credit is readily available to us for everything from furniture to electronics to automobiles ("Just 72 easy payments with zero down!"). As much as we know that *"the borrower is slave to the lender,"*[25] we still fall for it easily, do we not?

The best option is to become debt-free as quickly as possible. The least stressful way to make this happen is to have a solid, workable plan and stick to it. We include some resources for budgeting at the end of this chapter.

If debt is causing stress in your marriage, how are you addressing it?

No Written Budget

This is one of the most common causes of financial stress in a marriage that we have encountered—whether the annual income of a couple is barely five figures or into seven figures. Frankly, we are astounded by the number of marriages in which both husband and wife are unaware of how much money is coming into the family coffers or how much is going out.

Setting up a budget does not have to be an imposing or intimidating task. It does not have to be complicated at all. A budget is nothing more than a tool to help you see a monthly

---

[25] Proverbs 22:7b

picture of your finances. Once you know where you stand, you can make financial decisions that will help you walk together in harmony as a couple. This clarity is a powerful stress-reliever!

> *Once you know where you stand, you can make financial decisions that will help you walk together.*

Do you work with a written budget? If not, when are you going to set one up?

No Written Goals

Another source of stress is not having long-term financial goals regarding what your money can do for you. We recommend sitting down together and asking some questions of one other:

- What do we want our retirement to look like? Where will we live? What will we be doing with our time?
- If we have a mortgage, when do we want to be mortgage-free? What will being mortgage-free feel like? What will it do for us?
- What kind of vacations do we want to take? All-inclusive? Cruises? Oceanfront? Cottage life? Wilderness hikes? Skiing?
- If we have excess cash, what do we want to invest in? Real Estate? Stocks and bonds? Cryptocurrency? Precious metals? Other assets?

Once you have identified some long-term goals, reverse-engineer the process. Work backwards and break each goal down to short-term targets, say, 5-year goals, 1-year goals, monthly goals, weekly and daily goals.

For example, you want to celebrate your next milestone anniversary in Hawaii, 5 years from now. You estimate that a 2-week vacation in a condominium by the ocean will end up costing you $9,000. If you set aside $150 a month for 60 months, you can pay for that holiday debt-free. That could mean saving $35 a week that you are currently spending on eating out, entertainment, lottery tickets, lattés, or something else that is not essential, to reach the goal you have both set.

As usual, the key word in this process is *both*. When you are both involved in this process and make decisions together, you will have much less room for stress around managing your finances.

For larger goals such as retirement or becoming mortgage-free, we would highly recommend that you sit down with a financial planner. They can also help you save on taxes.

Have you written out or clearly discussed your financial goals?

Lack Of Transparency

This is a big one. We are consistently shocked by how many married couples do not offer full disclosure of their finances to their spouses. Though perhaps we shouldn't be so shocked, because it happened to us as well!

Since I (Jeeva) had settled in Canada before Sulojana arrived, I was used to making all the financial decisions on my own and handling all the banking, borrowing, saving, etc. Along the way, I started to take advantage of every credit card offer I received and built up quite a bulge in my wallet! In the beginning, when they were simply in my wallet, there was no harm done. But, as time went on and we had more month left than money, the credit cards started to come out of hibernation and into circulation.

Eventually I had racked up quite a large amount of credit card debt that I kept hidden from Sulojana. I managed to make the minimum monthly payments to keep the credit card companies happy, until the day of reckoning came, when I could not even make the minimum monthly payments. Now I started to see the dark side of the credit card companies. The same folks who were so happy to offer me membership privileges now made it clear that I had to pay up quickly to enjoy the perks! Finally, I had no choice but to let Sulojana see the ugly truth that I had been keeping under wraps for a long time. It was not a pretty scene.

I (Sulojana) was upset. Actually, I was furious, but I was also sad that he had not shared this with me earlier. I knew our finances weren't great, but I had no idea how bad! Unfortunately, similar stories unfold in many marriages even to this day. We have heard about secret bank accounts, unaccounted spending, gambling or other addictions, private loans given and taken—can you add to the list? All can cause enormous amounts of stress in a marriage. It certainly did in ours.

The good news was that once it was out in the open, Jeeva asked me to forgive him for the credit card spending and the lack of transparency. I was able to forgive him and together we came up with a plan to pay off all the debts. We are happy to report to you that we are totally debt-free now and well on our way to being mortgage-free too!

What financial "secrets" if any do you need to disclose to each other?

Action Step

> Share with each other any causes of financial stress you identified from the points above.

As you go through the next part of this chapter, ask yourself how the guidelines listed below can help you address these causes of stress.

ELIMINATING FINANCIAL STRESS

Here are five guidelines we put into place to help eliminate financial stress.

1. We had such differing philosophies and patterns of handling finances that we needed to work with a third party whom we both trusted and whose advice we would follow. For us, that person was Dave Ramsay. We took

his 10-session course, *Financial Peace University*,[26] at a local church. We immediately started implementing the "baby steps" that he teaches. We highly recommend him to all couples we mentor who are experiencing financial stress. Today we have our own personal financial consultant on retainer to provide us with a customized plan and offer counsel as needed.

2. We got into the habit of setting up a monthly written budget. To estimate the expenses accurately, we saved all our receipts for every purchase for 3 months. When we took the average of those expenses, our estimates were very close. We started using the "Allocated Expenses Plan"[27] template we picked up from Financial Peace University. We set up a monthly meeting to go over the budget. In our case, Jeeva filled in all the blanks on the template, then we would look at it together. This way we both knew exactly how much money was coming in that month and how much was going out. Total transparency.

We could easily tell if we were going to see a surplus at the end of the month or a deficit. If we noticed a deficit looming, then we would discuss how to avoid it, if possible. What expenses could we reduce or eliminate altogether? What could we do to bring in more income?

If it was a surplus, then the question was: What would we do with it? Pay down the principal on

---

[26] Learn more at ramseysolutions.com

[27] Free download available at ramseysolutions.com/budgeting/useful-forms

the mortgage? Replace old furniture? Take a trip? Increase our offerings that month? Or would we just leave it in a savings account until we could decide?

Once again, the key was both of us together making these decisions. When we did not have a written budget or the monthly meeting, one of us could spend money without knowing if our spouse had something else in mind for that amount. That would create unnecessary stress. After a while, we realized that it was good to do at least one mid-month check-up to assess how we were doing. It also helped us to see if anything new had come up that we needed to include.

3. We also established a maximum personal spending limit for each of us, i.e. an amount we could spend on our own without needing to check with the other. Of course, we would let the other person know when we did the spending, we just didn't have to ask ahead of time. We have kept it small, just $50. It works for us. No matter what the amount is, you will find it helps to set one and stick to it. Whenever one of us needs to spend more than $50 on a purchase, we will check to make sure that we both agree. Otherwise, we will not do it, even if it is on sale for the next 30 minutes only!

4. Another way that we have maintained transparency is by having joint bank and credit card accounts. Both our incomes go into a personal chequing account and all our expenses come out of the same account. We also have a joint savings account where we put away money for emergencies, 6 months' worth of expenses, future trips, retirement, etc. The same goes for credit cards: our

cards are in both our names. Since all accounts are joint, both of us can access any of them online at any given time to see what kind of activity has been going on.

As much as we recommend having joint accounts, we also know couples who manage their finances without stress by having separate accounts. In such cases, it is still important to maintain transparency by ensuring that both of you have access to each other's accounts. If one spouse really doesn't care to be involved in the financial planning, at least write down the account numbers and passwords so that if any disaster occurs to the financial planning spouse, the other can pick things up without any added headaches.

5. Ultimately, the main reason we have no stress in finances is because we trust God with our tithes and offerings. We stand on this promise:

> *"Will a man rob God? Yet you have robbed me...In tithes and offerings...Bring all the tithes into the storehouse...and try me now in this...if I will not open for you the windows of heaven, and pour out for you such blessing, that there will not be room enough to receive it. And I will rebuke the devourer for your sakes, so that he will not destroy the fruit of your ground..."* (Malachi 3:8–11 NKJV).

We honour God with our tithes and offerings, and as a result, we never worry about our finances. That said, it wasn't always this way. Jeeva grew up in a family that practised tithing, so it was natural for him. For Sulojana, it took some time to get used to tithing. Once we were on the same page, we joyfully gave our tithes and offerings, even when we were under a severe burden of debt. God kept His promises and brought us through those lean years. We would highly recommend you make tithes and offerings part of your monthly budget.

Finances are a common, though unnecessary, source of stress in a marriage. We hope that following these guidelines will help eliminate unnecessary financial stress from your marriage.

Action Steps

1. How did the guidelines listed above help you address the causes of financial stress you identified earlier?

2. What areas do you need to seek help from a professional?

3. Who are some people you can contact to get the help you need?

4. Who did you decide to work with?

   For additional discussion questions on this chapter, go to www.thesams.ca/resources or scan the QR code below:

CHAPTER 10

BOUNDARIES

If you have been diligently working your way through the process we have shared in this book, you should be well on your way to breakthrough by now. Congratulations if you have already reached that point! If not, no worries. It is coming. Keep on doing everything we have shared with you so far.

Regardless of your progress, you need to preserve and protect your marriage from the enemy's attempts to mess up all the good work that you have done. Picture your marriage as a house in a gated community. You need to put safeguards in place to make sure that your peace is not disturbed by outside forces that are hostile to you. Jesus describes the mission of the enemy in

> *Preserve and protect your marriage from the enemy's attempts to mess up all the good work that you have done.*

these words from John 10:10a: *"To kill, to steal and to destroy."* That is what Satan wants to do to your marriage as well.

A thief cannot enter your house and mess with your life when the security is as tight as it possibly can be. He can only enter through an opening that we provide, even if it is unwittingly—a door that is not locked, a window that is not shut properly, a security system that was not activated, etc. Similarly, the enemy of our souls will do his best to exploit any opening we provide. To prevent this from happening, we need to set boundaries and honour them diligently.

Before we get to the specific steps, let us look at the most common way that security is often compromised in a marriage.

TRIANGULATION

Triangulation is when a husband or a wife allows a third party to enter their marriage and form a triangle. This could potentially result in the strangulation of the marriage. You could say that triangulation is the combination of a triangle + strangulation.

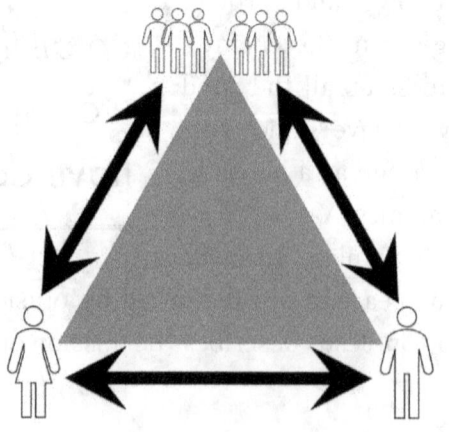

Triangulation can happen within the bounds of family relationships as well as outside. Here are some ways we have seen it make a mess of marriages.

Scenario 1

A husband is bent on purchasing a set of golf clubs. His wife is adamantly opposed to it. In frustration, she contacts a member of her family (mother, father, sister, sister-in-law, aunt, uncle—you pick) and vents. On one level, that may seem like a normal, natural thing to do. But what she has done is bring a third party into the marriage that did not need to be there.

A few days later, after some more back and forth dialogue between the spouses, self-reflection, and consideration of the family finances, the husband now decides that he is not going to get the golf clubs after all. He will wait until the end of the season or early spring when there are likely to be good deals available.

But the damage has been done. Everyone with whom she triangulated by sharing her sad saga is now privy to a "secret" that should have stayed between her and her husband. She willingly allowed access to uninvited guests whose view of the husband has now been poisoned, or at least tarnished by her sharing.

Scenario 2

A husband who is unhappy in his marriage attends his company's Christmas party, which his wife refused to attend.

He strikes up a conversation with a fellow employee from another department. His inhibitions and tongue loosened from a few glasses of wine, he starts sharing with her some of his frustrations with his wife. She listens patiently and sympathizes with his plight.

Early in the New Year, they run into each other in the company cafeteria, eat lunch together and share more of their hearts with each other. She is such a pleasant contrast to his wife! She dotes on every word he says, lets him talk as long as he wants to and makes him feel good! He enjoys the attention and senses an attraction to her. Gradually, he begins to develop an affection for her. Now they see each other every working day.

Shortly thereafter, his emotional adultery crosses over into the physical realm and he wants to leave his wife for this woman. See how triangulation is causing strangulation of a marriage? It could have been avoided had he realized what he was setting in motion by inviting a third party into their marriage.

Scenario 3

You had an unpleasant argument with your spouse, and you are extremely upset. You do not even want to call someone and tell them about it. So, you resort to the next best thing available: Electronic communication. It's EC! You fire off an angry e-mail about your spouse loaded with character assassination and trigger phrases such as: "He/She never…" "She/he always…" to chosen family members and friends who will be sympathetic to your version of events. Or you let your fingers do the talking as you convey the same information via text message.

You hurt so much that you want to inflict as much hurt as possible on the spouse who hurt you and as swiftly as humanly possible. Hello Facebook! You use Messenger if you have any measure of restraint. In the worst-case scenario, you write an angry post about it and tag some "key" allies who you know will take your side and agree with your assessment of your "enemy" spouse. Reading through their messages of support and emojis of care and anger makes you feel so vindicated!

The only problem of course is that once these digital messages are out there, they cannot be withdrawn. Sure, you can delete the post or retract an e-mail, but the damage has been done. Electronic communication is not easily destroyed and can almost always be retrieved. It is triangulation to the nth degree, raised to the power of infinity.

Similar scenarios are played every day by people who are unaware that these seemingly innocent interactions have serious consequences.

- A husband telling his secretary about how badly his wife treats him at home.
- A wife telling a friend about her husband's poor sexual performance.
- A husband telling a co-worker about his wife's spending habits.
- A wife telling her "best friend" sister-in-law about her husband's addictions.

These are just a few of the *"little foxes"* that will destroy your vineyard (Song of Solomon 2:15). Whenever you indulge in such behaviour, you are unwittingly inviting intruders into your intimate internal sanctuary—and that, dear spouses, is a definite no-no! If you want to not only preserve the victories you have won so far, but to keep on achieving greater levels of intimacy in your marriage, you need to stand on guard.

Action Step

> Confess to each other any instances of triangulation in your marriage—past and present. Use the process of reconciliation and the pattern of resolution from Chapter 6, as necessary.

INTERFERING IN-LAWS

In the Indian tradition, we are taught to honour anyone who is older, especially our parents, teachers, and other "elders" in our life. Upon getting married, our father and mother-in-law are added to the list. In India it is quite common for the newly married couple to live with the husband's parents. When one or both parents-in-law interfere in their child's marriage, this puts the couple in a precarious position. Many an Indian wife is caught between honouring her in-laws, loving her husband, and protecting herself from abuse—mental, emotional, verbal, and physical. Of course, this is not limited to the Indian culture, we are aware of families from many other cultures who also face similar dilemmas.

Regardless of the ethnicity, there are times when such tensions force a person to side with their parent(s) over their spouse, even in North America. This causes tension, stress, and conflict. Sadly, it could lead to a breach in the marriage and occasionally contribute to a break-up.

The guiding biblical principle for boundaries in this scenario is found in Genesis 2:24 (KJV): *"Therefore shall a man leave his father and his mother, and shall cleave unto his wife: and they shall be one flesh."* How does this apply? Godly parents-in-law who honour God's design must do nothing to shake or break the one-flesh-unity of their children's marriage. Married children honour their spouse as the #1 person in their life. They will not allow that privileged position to be occupied by anyone else, including their own parents.

Where there is interference by in-laws, we believe that it is up to the child whose parents are interfering to confront them and *"speak the truth in love"* (Ephesians 4:15). In a typical Indian family, the son takes the lead and ensures that his wife is not placed in a vulnerable position where she could be harmed by his parents' attitudes, words and/or actions. Please remember to forgive them first and frame your hurt using the "When you…I feel" formulation.

Do your best to obey Romans 12:18: *"If it is possible, as far as it depends on you, live at peace with everyone."* If it is not possible, and you are living under the same roof, you may wish to consider whether you ought to move out to honour God's "leave and cleave" directive. If you are living in separate locations, the two of you must come into agreement on the kind of boundaries you will maintain, such as how often you connect and for how long (e.g. visit once a month and stay for a day). You will also need to be alert when your parents resort to the "4 C's" (Criticizing, Condemning, Complaining or Comparing) about your spouse and stop it from getting worse.

> *Your spouse needs to know that you love them by the way you stand up for them.*

We recognize that this is easier said than done, but your spouse needs to know that you love them by the way you stand up for them in setting and sticking to boundaries with your parents. We also acknowledge that every situation is not as clear-cut as we have described it. Please seek the wisdom of God always and the counsel of trusted relationship experts, as necessary.

BOUNDARIES FOR YOUR MARRIAGE

Read through this list of boundaries that we have set for ourselves. Circle the ones you need to incorporate into your marriage.

- We will not talk to anyone else about our problems before talking to each other first.
  Jesus is very particular about this protocol: *"If your brother or sister sins against you, go to them. Tell them*

what they did wrong. Keep it between the two of you. If they listen to you, you have won them back. But what if they won't listen to you? Then take one or two others with you" (Matthew 18:15–16 GNT). Jesus is prescribing a code of conduct for believers within the church community, but when a husband and wife abide by it, can you see how "keeping it between the two of you" prevents triangulation from strangling your marriage?

- We will do everything in our power to solve problems "in-house."
  When we do share a problem with each other, we will first of all ensure that our spouse is open, willing and able to receive what we share without getting offended, flying off the handle or reacting in any other inappropriate manner. We will also be careful to use the "When you…I feel" formulation. After sharing, we will follow the steps to restoring peace. If we are not able to resolve it on our own, then and only then will we even consider talking to anyone else. We will do everything in our power to keep this process "in-house" before we take it to an outside party.

- We will share problems in our marriage only with a select few.
  We will share our "unresolvable" problems with a list of mutually agreed upon "neutral" people only—e.g. our pastor, a family member or friend we both trust, a counsellor or a mentor. We both need to be confident that these people will guarantee confidentiality and honour

our privacy. Furthermore, we will let our spouse know before we seek them out.

- We will only share positive things about our spouse publicly.
   Whatever we share about our personal lives with others will be of a positive nature. We will brag on each other's accomplishments, gestures of kindness and appreciation, even on social media. We will never share anything that will in any way come across as a put-down or belittling comment. We will resist the temptation to get a cheap laugh out of our spouse's quirks, missteps or mistakes, if it will embarrass them or make them look bad.

- We will not tolerate negative comments about our spouse by others.
   When we are faced with a situation where someone else starts talking negatively about our spouse, we will put an end to it right away by asking this question: "With your permission, I will share with my spouse what you just told me about her/him and name you as the source. Is that alright with you?" If they say "Yes", then we say: "OK, thanks for letting me know. I'll take it from here." If they say "Oh, no, please don't quote me!" we say: "OK, just so you know, I will not be bringing this up with him/her." In either event, the conversation goes no further.

- We will be totally transparent and vulnerable with each other about everything.

BOUNDARIES

We will not keep any secrets from each other. We will tell each other everything, so that there are no surprises (unless one of us is throwing a surprise party for the other... lol!) We have already covered some of this in previous chapters. We will share any addictions we struggle with or sins we have committed. We will have no secret bank accounts; both of us will have total unrestricted access to all financial details and matters. We will let the other person know if we breached the boundary and made a purchase above the maximum agreed amount.

In addition:

- We will let our spouse know of any symptoms or other health-related conditions we may be experiencing.

- We will make our spouse aware of any "inappropriate" contact anyone initiated with us—e.g. e-mails, texts, social media messages etc. from former boyfriends or girlfriends, ex-spouses or anyone else. We will always copy (cc) our spouse when we respond to any of them.

- We will not accept friend requests from our ex-es on social media or correspond with them for any reason other than to take care of matters pertaining to any children we may have in common.

- We will be extremely vigilant about our dealings with members of the opposite sex. We will do our best to avoid being in closed spaces (such as a vehicle) when alone with a person of the opposite sex. We will ensure that there is a third person present (of either sex), should the need arise for sharing a ride.[28] If we need to have a meal/drink with someone of the opposite sex for business purposes, networking, etc. we will meet in a public place and let our spouse know ahead of time where and when.

- Whenever the occasion calls for any kind of physical contact (e.g. hugs) with a member of the opposite sex, we will be careful to do it in such a way that is honourable and leaves no room for any misinterpretation of motives. Personally, we have chosen to reserve full-body hugs for family and close friends only.

- We will treat each other with respect, tenderness and honour. We will never use coarse, vulgar, or rude language when we talk to each other, even when an argument reaches boiling levels. We will take a timeout when necessary. We will not raise our voices, shout, or scream at each other for any reason. We will never treat each other with any physical force that causes

---

[28] We are aware that this so-called "Billy Graham" rule can be difficult to maintain in today's society. Author Danielle Strickland in her book, *Better Together*, points out how this has been used to protect men at the expense of women, therefore it needs to be re-examined. As far as we are concerned, this is a boundary that we have chosen to establish and are able to honour. As with any of these boundaries, you must consider the alternatives and decide on your own.

hurt. We will not push, pull, grab, or God forbid, hit our spouse or throw any objects at them.

- We will keep the marriage bed pure (Hebrews 13:4). We will inform each other about sexual advances anyone makes towards us and nip them in the bud. We will also confess if we have led someone else to believe that we are attracted to them sexually. We will focus only on our spouse when we are making love. If any other thoughts or images come, we will "H.A.L.T." them and take further steps as necessary to purify our minds. If one or both of us have given in to the temptation to watch pornographic images or videos, we will confess to each other first. Then we will seek the help we need to overcome this inclination or addiction. We will stay accountable to our spouse in addition to any other accountability partners.

- We will also be intentional about the content we watch, so that we do not allow impure images to enter our minds. We will do our best to vet what we plan to watch by checking reviews on sites such as movieguide.org. If despite our best efforts, something inappropriate shows up that we did not anticipate, we will have a quick conversation about whether we skip past that scene, keep watching or watch something else.

- We will confess our sins to each other (James 5:16). At the end of the day, we will check with each other to see if there is anything we have done that day that we need to confess, asking for God's forgiveness and each other's, where necessary.

- We will avoid the silent treatment as much as possible. We will take time to process our hurt and anger should we need it by calling a timeout. We will do our best to adhere to the Biblical principle stated in Ephesians 4:26b: *"Do not let the sun go down on your anger."* When we cannot get it taken care of before we sleep, we will do our very best to resolve it as quickly as possible the very next day. We will not let it linger and cast a shadow over our marriage.

Action Steps

Using this list of guidelines as a guide, write down the list of boundaries you would establish for your marriage. What boundaries do you think Jesus had? What more would you add?

CELEBRATE YOUR UNBREAKABLE MARRIAGE

Congratulations on working your way through *The Unbreakable Marriage*. We trust you used the companion workbook and maintained accountability with a mentoring couple all the way through.

Here are two ways we help couples who go through our Marriage Mentorship Process to celebrate.

1. With a meal at a fine restaurant of their choice. You too can follow suit. Enjoy being with each other. Share with each other how your life has been transformed since you started building your Unbreakable Marriage. What excites you about the future?

2. By renewing marriage vows. We generally serve as the officiants. You could ask your pastor, mentoring couple or someone else of your choice to preside. Here are the traditional vows we use. Feel free to use them or other set of vows that you exchanged at your wedding ceremony. Or write a new set of vows.

In the presence of God and before these witnesses,
I, ..., take you, ..., again,
to be my wife/husband,
to have and to hold
from this day forward,
for better for worse,
for richer or poorer,
in sickness and in health,
in joy and in sorrow,
to love and to cherish,
and to be faithful to you alone,
as long as we both shall live
(till death us do part).
This is my solemn vow.

Don't forget to kiss each other right after!

Your officiant may use the blessing on the next page or declare other words of blessing over you.

A BLESSING FOR YOUR MARRIAGE

May the Lord cause you to flourish, both you and your children. May you be blessed by the Lord, the Maker of heaven and earth (Psalm 115:15–16).

May you:
Love, honour and cherish each other, work together with one mind and purpose; forgive as the Lord forgave you and live in unity as one flesh.

May the God of peace make you holy in every way, and may your whole spirit and soul and body be kept blameless until our Lord Jesus Christ comes again (1 Thessalonians 5:23).

The Lord bless you and keep you.
The Lord make His face shine upon you and be gracious unto you.
The Lord lift up His countenance upon you and give you peace (Numbers 6:24–26 NKJV).

AFTERWORD: WHERE DO YOU GO FROM HERE?

If you are not yet ready to celebrate building your Unbreakable Marriage after going through this book and the companion workbook...

We would highly recommend that you receive personal, customized mentorship with us or another mentoring couple we have trained, over 12 weeks. This includes weekly sessions, mid-week checkups, unlimited inner healing sessions and 24/7 access to your mentors via email and text. 3 monthly follow-ups thereafter are also included. Results guaranteed or money back (conditions apply). By application only at www.thesams.ca.

We invite all of you to join our free Facebook group "The Unbreakable Marriage Community" where you can interact with other readers of this book and encourage one another. We will also be posting more teachings, updates and information on exclusive events you can attend to take your marriage to greater heights in that group. Go to www.facebook.com/groups/theunbreakablemarriage or scan the QR code below right now.

ADDITIONAL READING & RESOURCES

We have found the following books and online resources helpful, and recommend them for further research, growth and healing.

On Soaking:
Soaking in the Spirit by Carol Arnott
Soaking Encounter Journal by Carol Arnott

On forgiveness:
Grace and Forgiveness by John & Carol Arnott
Forgiving What You Can't Forget by Lysa TerKeurst
The Art of a Genuine Apology by Andrew Blackwood

On communication:
Keep Your Love On by Danny Silk
Laugh your way to a healthy marriage by Mark Gungor

On parental blessings:
Blessing Generations by Craig Hill
Relentless Generational Blessings by Arthur Burk
The Family Blessing Guide by Terry & Melissa Bone

On sexuality:
Come As You Are by Emily Nagoski
The Great Sex Rescue by Sheila Wray Gregoire, Rebecca Gregoire Lindenbach and Joanna Sawatsky

On pornography:
The Last Relapse by Sathiya Sam
Unwanted by Jay Stringer
xxxChurch.com

On romance:
Date Night Journal by Monica Tanner

Inner Healing resources:
The *Sozo* Inner Healing ministry – bethelsozo.com
Restoring The Foundations – https://www.restoringthefoundations.org/
Neil Anderson's *Bondage Breakers* – ficm.org
Soul Beliefs by Tammy Hernandez
Soul-Healing Love by Drs. Tom & Beverley Rodgers

On Finances:
Prosperous Home by Stephen K. De Silva
The Total Money Makeover by Dave Ramsey

ADDITIONAL READING & RESOURCES

On Transforming Marriage:
Love After Marriage by Barry & Lori Byrne
The Wife Revolution by Sandra Arcadipane

On the prophetic:
Translating God by Shawn Bolz

To request a prophetic word:
fathersheartministry.net/request-prophetic-word
unvale.com.au/receive-a-word

ACKNOWLEDGMENTS

While we can claim that the outline of our marriage mentorship is original to us, we cannot take sole credit for creating the entire process. We gratefully acknowledge many leaders in the Body of Christ whose books, videos, workshops, mentorship, and impartation have influenced us. We have been diligent to acknowledge the few who graciously granted us permission to reproduce their materials. However, there are likely many others whose influence permeates this process without us even being aware of it. We are grateful to God for placing you in our paths. You too share in the reward we get to see of marriages saved and lives transformed.

We especially wish to thank:

John & Carol Arnott for their blessing and permission to use stories and prayers from their amazing book *"Grace & Forgiveness."*

Arthur Burk of the Sapphire Leadership Group for allowing us to use the Spirit Blessing, taking the time to read through what we wrote and approving it.

Barry & Lori Byrne of Nothing Hidden Ministries, who opened our eyes to see how quickly the Holy Spirit can turn marriages around. Attending their Love After Marriage and Spirit Connection workshops blessed our marriage immensely and gave us resources that have blessed couples in our marriage mentorship.

Matt & Lisa Tapley, Senior Pastors at Lakemount Worship Centre in Grimsby, Ontario for granting us permission to use their meaty message on marriage, "*Bold Love*".

Ruth Teakle, also from Lakemount, for her invaluable input into the section on Removing Spiritual Blockages.

Steve & Sandra Long, Senior Leaders of Catch The Fire Toronto, who are our spiritual parents, for all they have taught, prayed, released and imparted to us over the years.

Sean Mize, our coach, who recommended that we write a book to share our message and method with the rest of the world.

Perry Marshall, marketing expert, who has provided valuable counsel through the various stages of the writing and publishing journey.

ACKNOWLEDGMENTS

Ron Mills, for inspiring the pictorial depiction of the spirit-soul-body connection.

Steven Kasyanenko for sharing the vision that turned into the striking cover graphic.

Krysta Koppel, for the graphics sprinkled throughout the book.

Jonathan Puddle, our editor, for the tremendous role he played in the evolution of this book. Incorporating his recommendations for revising the original draft has made the book wholesome and holistic in a way we could not have imagined.

Our many volunteer readers, proofreaders and Melissa Bone, who painstakingly went through the manuscript and spotted errors, alerted us to passages that were unclear and helped us make the book more readable.

Many who have prophesied about us writing a book.

Last, but not least, all the couples who trusted us enough to invest in our Marriage Mentorship Process. We appreciate how we were able to test, validate and refine the process from where we began to where it is today, because of your willing participation. Special thanks to those couples who graciously gave us permission to include their testimonies in this book.

ABOUT THE AUTHORS

JEEVA AND SULOJANA SAM are marriage mentors based in Ontario, Canada. Jeeva retired in 2017 after 35+ years as a pastor. Sulojana has worked for the Government of Canada since 2007. They reside in the Niagara Region of Canada.

The Sams are celebrating the 39th anniversary of their arranged marriage in 2022. They are parents of three married children--Priya and her husband, Duncan, Sathiya and his wife Shaloma and Jaya and his wife Rachel.

They were one of three couples featured on 100 Huntley Street's 40 Day Love Dare Challenge in 2010. This experience eventually led them to create a process which guarantees breakthrough for couples facing breakdown in as little as 10 weeks.

The Sams strongly believe that no matter how broken a marriage may be, it can be restored when BOTH husband and wife commit themselves to do whatever it takes to make it work. Once they learn how to access the power of God, apply the sound biblical principles and use the tools in this book, they are certain to turn their marriage around.

Jeeva and Sulojana are on a mission to save 50,000 marriages from divorce in the next 5 years. Your marriage could be one of them!

Reach out to them and get the help you need by visiting www.thesams.ca or by e-mail: theunbreakablemarriage@gmail.com.

Connect with them on social media:
Facebook: @theunbreakablemarriagebook
Instagram: @theunbreakablemarriage

Join The Unbreakable Marriage Community at www.facebook.com/groups/theunbreakablemarriage or by scanning this QR code:

www.ingramcontent.com/pod-product-compliance
Lightning Source LLC
Chambersburg PA
CBHW072049110526
44590CB00018B/3098